THE HEALING OF WINDWALKER

A Story of Love, Hate and Redemption

DONALD L CHADD

CITIOFBOOKS, INC.
3736 Eubank NE Suite A1
Albuquerque, NM 87111-3579
www.citiofbooks.com
Hotline: 1 (877) 389-2759
Fax: 1 (505) 930-7244

Ordering Information:

Quantity sales. Special discounts are available on quantity purchases by corporations, associations, and others. For details, contact the publisher at the address above.

Printed in the United States of America.

ISBN-13:   Softcover   979-8-89391-109-1
                eBook   979-8-89391-110-7

Library of Congress Control Number: 2024909651

TABLE OF CONTENTS

ACKNOWLEDGMENTS

This book could not have been written without the help of many special people. I'd like to thank my dear friend, Greg Tullet, for the many hours he spent putting my written thoughts into readable order and for refining certain elements of the plot. I also want to thank my wonderful wife, Laurie, for the time she took out of her busy schedule to read and re-read the manuscript and offer me her opinions and suggestions.

I owe a debt of gratitude to a number of friends whose comments, questions, and suggestions have improved this book immeasurably.

Thank you all!

AUTHOR'S NOTES

The writing of this book was a labor of love because it is based on the true life stories and events in not only my own life, but the lives of my family members and friends as well. Five of these friends have had life-after-death experiences and their stories are presented here as part of the life and death experiences of my fictitious main character, "Windwalker". I have wrapped my life history around him which made this story very personal to me.

The book also includes much Native American history and lore and I have made every effort to be as authentic as possible. As it was told to me.

The inspiration for writing this book came as a result of my long association with Native Americans, and in particular, one Navajo gentleman with whom I had the pleasure to dine a number of years ago. During the course of our evening together, we had a discussion about things that were happening on the reservation. He shared with me, among other things, that it was his opinion that the Native Americans will never come into their own as a people until they "lay down the false traditions of their fathers and take up the true traditions of the ancient ones." The ancient ones history can be found in "The Book of Mormon: Another Testament of Jesus Christ". This book is a result of the many years I pondered, prayed and researched about what that statement actually means.

Disclaimer: The information and conclusions in this book are not endorsed, sponsored by, or affiliated with The Church of Jesus Christ of Latter-day Saints or any other group or individual. All the information in the book came from information I gathered from original conversations with many different individuals over many years.

Dedication

For my wife, Laurie Chadd

My brother and sisters: Bob, Kathy, Nancy and Joyce My Mom and Dad, Harold and Dorothy Chadd My grandparents,

Rex and Marie Marsh; Jim and Liddy Chadd

My aunts and uncles, especially, Betty Watson.

INTRODUCTION

My name is Richard George, and I have been given a sacred trust. I had been serving as a bishop in The Church of Jesus Christ of Latter-day Saints for about four years when my wife developed ovarian cancer and subsequently died. The overwhelming sense of loss I felt made it necessary for me to retire as CEO of an international mining company, and to take a break from my many church responsibilities. I felt I needed time alone to commune with God and to find answers to several questions that had been troubling me. After pondering and praying about where to go, I was drawn to the rugged beauty of the mesas in the Four Corners area of Colorado where I had hunted many times over the years.

One day, while I was exploring the top of a mesa, I came upon an old Indian man sitting alone as if in prayer. He didn't stir as I approached, and I wondered whether or not I should disturb him. I was extremely concerned about his condition, but when I tried to persuade him to let me help him get medical attention, he told me that he had seen a vision and already knew he was going to die there on the mesa. He said that in his vision, he was told that a man would be sent to him before he died to help him accomplish his mission here on earth. He told me that I was that man and he had been waiting for me. He then proceeded to relate to me the most amazing story I have ever heard! However, the story was nothing compared to the astonishing vision I had just prior to his demise in which I was taught the great mysteries of life after death. Having had this extraordinary experience, I am now able to relate to you his completed story and the powerful message he was destined to deliver to his people, and ultimately to the world.

PART ONE

CHAPTER 1

WINDWALKER

My name is Windwalker Chad Smith, better known as "Walker," and I was born in the Four Corners area of Colorado. There is a story attached to my name, which will be made known to you as you listen to my tale. My mother was a reservation Indian who, I thought, had no family. She also had major problems with alcohol, so she wasn't able to take care of me when I was born. One day she took me to a neighbor's eight-year-old daughter and asked her to take care of me for an hour, and she never came back to get me. The girl's parents would have kept me, but their daughter refused to change diapers or to help take care of me. Consequently, they had no other choice than to turn me over to the tribe who then had to find a new home for me. The tribal elders looked all over the reservation for my mother but were unable to find her. That's how I became part of the "system." Apparently they found someone who was willing to change my diapers because someone took care of me for a while until a permanent home could be found.

The first thing I can remember was leaving one foster home and going to another one. I think I must have been about three years old then. Over time I was placed in several different homes. Most of my foster parents were nice, but others weren't so nice, and some were just downright mean. It took me awhile, but I figured out how to get along with most of them. The hardest ones to get along with were the ones who had children because they blamed me for everything that went wrong even when it was their own children's fault. I found this to be an impossible situation. My anger and resentment grew until all I wanted was to get revenge. I soon learned that I could get even with not only the parents but also with their children. Even though I was little I knew how to make their lives pure hell, and I did.

I was almost ready to start school, and the only name I had ever been known by was "The Kid." I don't know why, but I hated that name! No matter what I did, I couldn't get anyone to stop calling me The Kid! I wondered why everyone else had regular names and I didn't.

One day I heard someone telling a story about a great warrior who had a magnificent horse. The horse was the source of the warrior's greatness and power, so everyone wanted to own him. I was very small and afraid of horses, but for some reason I loved hearing that story. As I listened, I tried to hear what the warrior's name was. Even though I was too young to know what a warrior was, I knew that I had to know his name. At first I couldn't understand what they were calling him, and it wasn't until almost the end of the story that I figured out that his name was Windwalker. I knew that name fit me perfectly! After all the time I had been called The Kid, I realized that it had been for a purpose, because now I was able to choose my own name. From now on it would be Windwalker.

I remember watching all the other kids going to school on the school bus and I couldn't wait for my turn to come. I could hardly think of anything else. I stood by the bus stop every morning and evening and watched all the kids getting on and off the bus. They seemed to be having so much fun laughing and playing with each other. Where I was living, no one ever wanted to play with me. They just yelled at me and told me to get out of the house.

One day, as I headed toward the bus stop to watch the kids getting off the bus, I was confronted by a dark-haired fat man and a nicely dressed blonde lady. "Are you Windwalker?" the fat man asked me. "Yes," I said. "And who are you?" "I represent your tribe, and now that you are five years old, it's time for you to start school. This is Mrs. Smith, and she would like you to stay with her and her family this next year while you go to school. Please come with us so you can pick up your things." The family I lived with was so mean to me that I only went to their house when I was hungry or when someone made me. I really hated living there!

When we got to the house, the pretty lady made me sit on her lap. I remember how good she smelled, and in a short time I was actually enjoying being there. She and Fat Man were talking about something called the "Indian Placement Program." I knew that I was an Indian, but the word "placement" frightened me. Even though I liked the pretty lady, I wasn't going to let anyone placement me, so I started to make plans to find some food and run away. Food was very important to me because I never had enough to eat and was always hungry. Since I had been in a lot of new homes, and most of the time it wasn't good, I wanted to run and hide, but I couldn't because the lady was holding me too close! Usually I would have been kicking, fighting, and biting to get away, but I realized that I actually liked her holding me.

Then I was told to get my things so we could go to my new home. I didn't have much, so it only took me a couple of minutes. Before we got into the car I remembered I had forgotten my coat, and since I didn't want to go back to the house, I decided to leave it. I couldn't believe how clean the car was and how good it smelled! That was the first time I had ever been in a clean car, and I really liked it. The lady held me in her lap and I soon fell asleep. I slept for a long time, and when I woke up, we had stopped at a place to eat. I had never seen so much food before! I just sat there looking at it until the lady asked me if I was hungry. I had always been told what to eat and when I could eat. But she told me I could eat as much as I wanted of anything on the table, so I started shoveling food into my mouth as fast as I could before she changed her mind. I had never tasted anything so good! Some of the food was even sweet! I was starting to like that lady more and more. She told me her name was Kathy, and then she asked me what my real name was. She looked at me as though she didn't believe me when I told her my real name was Windwalker, which was so upsetting to me that I refused to say another word to her during the rest of the trip. We finally got to the lady's house, and the fat man dropped us off there. Little did I know then how much I would grow to fear and to hate that man.

I couldn't believe how beautiful my new home was! There was lots of green grass and pretty flowers in the yard, but the most beautiful flowers of all were called "roses." Then, to my absolute horror, everything fell apart! She had lots children, so I immediately knew that this arrangement wasn't going to work. I had never been able to get along in any family that had children. Some how though, this was different because they actually seemed excited to see me. They were all laughing and hugging me, and they wanted to show me my room. I never had a bedroom before, so I was amazed! The room, which I would be sharing with another boy, had two beds in it, one on top of the other. They asked me which one I wanted, and even though I wanted the top one, I didn't say anything. Then, to my great relief, all but one of the children left to go to their own homes. They had just come over to meet me and to welcome me. The boy who stayed was named Robbie. He appeared to be about three years old, and little did I know then what an important role he would play in my life.

Soon I was told it was bath time. I hated baths because the water was always dirty and cold, but here the bath was different. It was hot and had a lot of bubbles in it. After my bath it was suppertime. I had my own chair, and there was lots of food. I grabbed the first thing within reach and started eating as fast as I could. All of a sudden, I noticed that no one was eating and the whole family was looking at me. Then Kathy's husband, Buddy, said it was time for prayers. I was told to cross my arms, close my eyes, and bow my head. Even though that was when someone back home would have hit me, for some reason I felt safe and did as I was told, except for closing my eyes. Then everyone said "Amen" and they all started eating. That was many years ago. Even though I was five years old at the time I can remember it like it happened yesterday. Before bed we gathered around Kathy as she read to us. Then, to my delight, we had a tickle game. Next, we had to brush our teeth. They gave me a toothbrush and showed me how to use it. I remember that the toothpaste tasted so good I started eating it and everyone laughed at me. Normally that would have made me mad, but this time I laughed along with them. Everyone acted as though they were being tickled all the time, and I knew I was going to get to like that way of life.

When I went into my room, Robbie was sitting in his little chair. He told me to pick which bed I wanted to sleep on and said I could try both of them if I wished. I chose the top, and I remember that I couldn't go to sleep because I was afraid someone would come and get me during the night to take me to another family. All I knew was that

I wanted to stay there. The next morning when Robbie and I got up, we made our beds and cleaned our room. I was the star attraction as the whole family stood around watching me try to make my bed. Since I was little and my bed was high, it was very difficult for me to get the covers where they were supposed to go. Robbie told me later on that he was very glad I had chosen the top bunk, for obvious reasons.

The next morning everyone gathered around the table and read from the scriptures before breakfast. Even though Robbie was a couple of years younger than I was he was able to read quite well. It was then I made up my mind that I was going to become as good a reader as everyone else. Kathy assured me that she would teach me, and I was eager to get started. Later in the afternoon, Kathy took me shopping for school clothes. She even bought me underwear! Since I had never owned underwear before, this was a whole new experience for me. I decided I really liked my new underwear and I took every opportunity to run around in it with nothing else on.

Soon, I was attending the first grade, which I loved! Kathy helped me with my learning and all the kids played with me. It was so fun when we went to the park and when Buddy stayed home and we read the scriptures and played games. On Sundays we all went to church together, which I thoroughly enjoyed. I loved my life! We all had our chores, and I tried hard to do a good job. I knew Kathy and Buddy loved me and appreciated my efforts.

Then school was over for the summer, and Robbie and I spent our first day of vacation playing in the park. Since most of the kids in the neighborhood were there, we chose sides and played cowboys and Indians. I was always the chief and everyone followed me.

When we got home, Fat Man and two strange women were waiting for me. They told me it was time for me to go back to the reservation for the rest of the summer. I started to cry, and I couldn't stop. Several of my friends were there with me, and they were crying too. We all ran to my room and crawled under the bed to hide from those bad people. We decided we needed to block the door, so we jammed a chair up under the doorknob to make sure that no one was going to be able to open the door. I was even afraid to get close to the window for fear that someone would be able to grab me from outside. My friends said they would protect their chief and refused to leave the room. Kathy and Buddy had to let my friends' parents know what was going on, and the parents brought some treats to draw us out, but it didn't work. There was no way we were going to open that door! I was really scared, and I didn't know what to do. All I knew was that I didn't want to leave Kathy, Buddy, Robbie, and my friends because I was sure that they would forget about me and I would never see them again. I felt so helpless! The one thing I did know was that they were not going to take me away from there! Kathy and Buddy talked to Fat Man for a long time, and all of a sudden I could hear Kathy and Buddy saying, "Thank you, thank you, oh, thank you!" Then Fat Man and the ladies left the house and drove away. Evidently Fat Man couldn't find my mother and no one knew who my father was. Also, no one on the reservation wanted me, and since no one wanted me, they said I could stay with Kathy and Buddy. Kathy and Buddy were laughing and crying and thanking God, and I found myself doing the same. At that point in my life, I didn't really know who God was, but I was grateful to him anyway. When the crisis was over, we tried to open the door, but we had jammed the chair so tightly under the doorknob we couldn't get it loose. Buddy tried to open the window, but the room had been painted, and the window had been painted shut, so we couldn't get the window to open either. We realized that we were trapped in the room, so Buddy ended up having to break the window to get us out. The next day he freed up all the windows so they would open.

Buddy and Kathy told me that Robbie was adopted and that they would do everything in their power to adopt me too. That way nobody would ever be able to take me away from them.

After a really fun summer vacation, I started second grade. Kathy helped me with all of my schoolwork, so I knew more than anyone else in my class. My teachers always called on me because I always knew the answers. It was great! And Kathy was really terrific! I didn't know why, but Kathy and Buddy weren't allowed to adopt me that year either. They figured it was the tribe that wouldn't allow the adoption. I really didn't care as long as I could stay with Kathy, Buddy, and Robbie.

Third grade was the greatest of all because of football! I was fast, and once I got that ball, no one could get it away from me. Since I had so many things taken from me when I was little, I was bound and determined not to let anybody take "my ball." Every time I made a goal, I jumped into the air and yelled, "My ball, my ball, my ball." When I was going for the ball, I could hear Kathy shouting "They have your ball, go get it," and I got it no matter what it took.

During my fourth grade year, we moved to a mining town called Uravan because Buddy owned some underground uranium mines. Since I was good in sports, I had no problem making new friends. I thought Uravan was a funny name for a town, so I asked Kathy about it. She told me that since the people mined uranium and vanadium there, they put the first part of the two words together and came up with Uravan. We moved into small houses called the "Flat Tops," which were like apartments. Four families lived in each Flat Top. I remember one mom baking pies and placing them on her window sill to cool. One day one of us kids, and there were a lot of kids in Uravan, stole one of her pies. We ran, but I was the one who got caught. She was pretty nice about the theft and told me that if we wouldn't steal any more of her pies, she would bake one especially for us kids. The only stipulation was that we had to wait for the pie to cool and then get her permission before taking it. The wait was always worth it, and it wasn't long before she had to bake more than just one pie for all of us.

I have so many memories of Uravan! It was there I became aware that my dog, Scotty, was my protector. When the other kids and I played football, we had to tie Scotty up or he would attack anyone who touched me. One day Buddy had to give me a spanking, and after the first swat, Scotty charged him, tearing Buddy's skin wide open. The next time I needed a spanking, Buddy made sure that Scotty was outside with the door closed! Unfortunately, the windows were wide open, so when I received that first swat, Scotty heard it. He jumped through a window and took Buddy again! This time it was worse than the last time. Buddy and Kathy talked for a long time about getting rid of Scotty, but in the end it was decided that it was good for me to have a protector. They told me they would be sure the windows and doors were closed the next time I got a spanking. Come to think of it, I don't remember getting another spanking after that.

With Scotty at my side, I was the toughest kid on the block. One day some of the neighborhood boys built a fort behind the houses. They dug a trench and covered it with branches and dirt to make a tunnel. I wanted to play with them, but because I wasn't a member, they wouldn't let me in. That made me mad, so I decided to claim the fort and kick them out. All three of them were ready to fight, but they kept looking at Scotty. Finally one of the boys said, "Okay, you can have the fort, but if it wasn't for that dog, we would kick your ——!" I just smiled at them and said, "But I do have the dog, so beat it!" They took off running. Unfortunately I didn't get to keep the fort for long because they told their parents what had happened. The parents checked out the fort and said it was too dangerous, and they tore it down.

In the fifth grade, I found out that the boy delivering the *Denver Post* was going to high school, so he wouldn't be able to deliver papers anymore. I asked Kathy and Buddy if I could take his place. They said I wouldn't be able to because I didn't have a bicycle and it was too far to go get one. I started looking for a used bike and found what we later called the "Blue Bomb." It was an old bike that didn't have fenders, and the chain wouldn't stay on. The tires wobbled so badly you couldn't even ride it, so Buddy replaced some parts and tightened the spokes and got it working pretty well. The only problem was that it was too big for me. If I sat on the seat, my feet didn't reach the bicycle pedals. If I sat on the crossbar, I could reach the pedals but I couldn't get back up onto the seat. Since Buddy was great at figuring things out, I knew that he would come up with a solution to the problem, and he did. He taped pieces of a two-by-four onto the pedals so I would be able to pedal the bike and sit on the seat at the same time. The only major problem was that if a pedal turned over, I could no longer reach it while sitting on the seat! I wondered what the answer to the dilemma was, but once again, Buddy had a solution. He put pieces of two-by-four on both sides of the pedals and I was ready to deliver papers! I had two saddlebags full of papers and was ready to go until I discovered that when I made a sharp turn, the bottom two-by-four dug into the dirt and the bike flipped over. That caused me to take some real nasty spills, so I finally ended up ditching the bike and walking my route with my saddlebags over my shoulders. I sold so many papers the *Denver Post* rewarded me with a trip to Lakeside Theme Park, in Denver. I never won another contest for selling the most papers because, by that time, I was delivering the paper to almost everyone in town.

Buddy told me that when he was in school, he got paid for helping the janitor move desks. So, I decided to ask my school janitor if he would pay me to help him move desks. He said he would. One day a skunk was trapped in one of the school trash cans and I got an idea. I remembered that awhile back Buddy had mentioned that a skunk had gotten into his school and sprayed. He said no one could go to school for a whole week! I figured the kids would think I was a hero if the skunk sprayed in the school, so I chased the skunk through all of the classrooms and even into the principal's office. When the janitor saw what I had done, he almost had a heart attack! The next day I was expecting a hero's reception at school, but what I got was a trip to see the principal. His office really stunk! The principal was so mad he wouldn't let us out of school for even a day. Every hour the janitor sprayed some horrible-smelling stuff around the school that was even worse than skunk smell. All the kids hated me, and they shunned me that whole week. As if that wasn't bad enough, I also lost my desk-moving job!

Buddy always helped me when I wanted to do something. When I wanted to take care of lawns while people went on vacation, he helped me get hand clippers so I could trim the grass. He also helped me buy a lawn mower. I had a lot of work, and I had a lot of money. I was able to buy a baseball bat, balls, a bow and arrows, and even a gun.

In sixth grade, we had a new principal whose name was Bear Hunter. He was an Indian, and his skin, hair, and eyes were dark like mine. Bear Hunter had a little girl who walked to school with us. She was very quiet, and the other kids made fun of her, which made her cry. I liked her and would sometimes walk her home, but she never spoke to me. She didn't play out with the other kids, and it seemed to me that she was very sad. I don't think she wanted to stay there anymore, and I felt sorry for her. One day Kenny, Johnny, and I were walking down the road, and she was walking in front of us. Along came two boys who started pulling her hair and throwing rocks at her. We ran them off, but she was crying so hard she couldn't see where she was going.

We took her home, and when we got there, her mother met us at the door. She was angry and told us to get out of there and never to bother her daughter again. She slammed the door on us before we could say anything.

The next day, the principal called us out of our classroom, which was located in the basement of a separate building that housed a theater and a basketball court. He took us upstairs and started to cuss at us and accuse us of hurting his daughter. We tried to tell him that it wasn't us and that all we did was to take her home. He started screaming at us and calling us liars, so I jumped up and told him that he was a liar and not us. Instantly, he exploded and hit me so hard he knocked me to the floor. He grabbed the other two boys, slammed them up against the wall, and started slapping them. I got up and grabbed his arm to stop him, and he slapped me so hard I wet my pants. I noticed that the other boys had wet their pants too. Just as fast as he had started beating us, he stopped and said he was sorry. We told him, again, that we didn't hurt his daughter and that we had only walked her home because she was crying so hard she couldn't see where she was going. He started crying and asked us if we would forgive him. I didn't know men could cry, but he sure did! We felt sorry for him, so we said that everything was okay. He told us we didn't have to go back to class until after lunch, and he allowed us to play basketball until lunch time, which was really great!

At noon I went out front to wait for Buddy because he always picked me up and took me home for lunch. Buddy was waiting there just like he always was. He looked at me and asked, "What's wrong with your eyes?" I stood there not knowing what to say. He slowly got out of the car and looked at me. Even though my pants were almost dry, he could tell they had been wet. Then he asked me if I had been crying, and I knew if I said anything, I had to tell him the truth. You couldn't lie to Bud dy because he knew everything, so I clammed up and didn't say anything. As far as I was concerned, everything was fine because Bear Hunter had said he was sorry and had let us play basketball all morning instead of going back to class. Buddy then asked me if I had wet my pants, and again, I clammed up and didn't say anything. He was puzzled and asked me why I wouldn't tell him what had happened. We stood there just looking at each other for what seemed like an eternity. Then, without saying a word, Buddy turned toward the car, slowly walked over to it, and opened the door.

As Walker related that incident to me, he appeared to be exhausted by the memory of it. He told me that he needed to stop for a while because the experience he would relate to me next was one of the most frightening experiences of his childhood. He said that before he could tell me about the experience, he would have to tell me more about Buddy and Kathy so I could understand the horror of what was going to happen next. I suggested that he rest while I fixed us some lunch. He expressed his gratitude and told me that he would continue his story after lunch.

CHAPTER 2

BUDDY

After we had eaten, I could see that Walker was feeling better. He sat up and returned to his recollections.

Buddy's parents were teachers, and he was the older of two sons. When World War II started, Buddy was one of the first to join. He and his parents had loved going hunting and fishing together, and over the years Buddy honed his tracking skills to the point where he could read signs in nature that no one else could even see. His rifle was like a part of his arm. He could take any gun, and after the first shot, he knew how the gun was shooting. From that point, he could put three bullets into the center of the target so close together that all three holes were touching. He used to have fun with our friends because they heard three shots and saw what looked like only one hole. They thought two of the bullets missed the target. They didn't know how anyone could shoot three bullets through the same hole.

At this point, Walker had to pause because of a bad coughing spell. His hands shook as he wiped his mouth. I noticed a trace of blood. When he recovered, we continued.

That was what I loved about going shooting with him. Our friends couldn't believe that there were three holes in the same place, so he would show them by taking one shot at a time. After he fired each shot, we used a piece of tape to cover up the hole. I loved doing this because I was the one to retrieve the target, and we could see where the bullet went through the tape in almost the same place as the first one. But the third shot was the best one! After retrieving the target, I loved seeing the look of surprise and amazement in our friends' eyes when they saw another hole right where the last one had been.

From the time I started living with Kathy and Buddy, Buddy took Robbie and me along with him when he went hunting. It must have looked funny, the great hunter being followed by two little boys. Robbie and I were so small that sometimes we would get high-centered on logs that were lying in our way. When I finally got my first gun, Buddy took me hunting. Buddy was going to shoot the deer, and I was going to shoot the rabbits. As we crept through the woods, all I could think about was finding a rabbit. I had seen rabbits in the past and remembered how fast they could run. The more I thought about it, the more I realized that if I had to take the safety off before shooting a rabbit, I might not be fast enough and the rabbit would get away. So I took the safety off. At the next deadfall, Buddy stopped and turned while straddling a log. He asked me if my gun was on safety. I said it was. I knew Buddy could sense when people were lying, but I tried it anyway. He looked at me for what seemed like a long time, which made me so uncomfortable I almost confessed. At that moment he told me to pull the trigger. My heart almost stopped! I had no choice but to pull the trigger. I was so thankful that I was carrying the gun on my shoulder so it wasn't pointing at anyone! I used my left hand to pull the trigger and it went off. Looking back, I admire how Buddy dealt with it. He took my gun, unloaded it by ejecting the shells onto the ground, and without his saying a word we returned to our truck. We continued in silence all the way home. He put my gun up on his bedroom shelf where it stayed for the rest of the entire year.

Buddy's hunting license allowed us to get three deer each season. He would always get two dry does and one big buck. The does were for steaks and roasts. The big buck was for sausage and mince meat pies. My classroom at school had a little window in the door, and during hunting season I would hear a little knock on the window and there would be Buddy looking through the glass. I knew that he had gotten a big buck and needed help getting it out. When he went for his buck, he had to go into some deep canyons and forest where the big game was. Sometimes it took two or three days to get the buck home and dressed out.

When tracking game, I swear Buddy was like a walking ghost. He made absolutely no sound; it was almost like he was floating. One day when I was following him, he kept telling me to walk quietly. I got a little upset and decided that I would stop for a minute so he would realize that I wasn't the only one making noise. I stopped and stood still while he moved around the oak brush. The next thing I knew, I heard his voice directly behind me saying, "Are you coming?" I never heard him come up behind me! After that, I did my best to be quiet during the rest of the hunt.

I remember that on Fridays, if we smelled chicken frying when we got home from school, we knew we were either going fishing or hunting. When Buddy went to check on his mines, he always gave me a box of shells, put me in the back of the pickup, and off we went. The mines had waste dumps of rocks that didn't have any ore in them, but rabbits loved to live there. While he checked out the mines, I got the meat for supper. We boys were his shadow. Buddy had a real neat saying, "It doesn't hurt to spoil a child if they mind," and he spoiled us! I did everything I could to mind him.

As I mentioned before, Buddy served in World War II. He had been given some special assignments because of his ability to shoot and track. Buddy's brother told me that Buddy's job was to kill people. He said he killed a lot of people, and most of them he had killed with his knife and bare hands. I asked Buddy about this a lot of times, but he didn't want to talk about the war. It wasn't until sometime later that I fully realized the damaging effects the war had had on him.

Shortly after I went to live with Buddy and Kathy, we went to a movie. After the movie, Robbie and I were laughing and running around Kathy playing tag with her. Buddy was following a short distance behind watching us. All of a sudden a car backfired and with lightning speed, he grabbed me by my shirt and threw me into a trash can. Then he grabbed Robbie by the arm, wrapped his arm around Kathy's waist, slammed her to the ground and covered her and Robbie with his body. He did all of that in about a split second! Robbie's shirt was ripped all the way down the back and his arm was really hurt. Kathy's face was bleeding from being pushed into the pavement, and her arms and legs were also bleeding. Luckily for me, I was unhurt. This is what the war did to Buddy. He had flashbacks for years following the war. Later, Robbie liked to tease me about Buddy's throwing me away in the trash.

Sometimes Buddy had bad dreams. These dreams were so bad that he soaked the bed with sweat. When this happened, he would tremble and shake so badly that he couldn't walk. One time when Kathy tried to wake him up, he hit her so hard he gave her two black eyes. We learned to stay away from him when he had those dreams, until he could wake himself up. When he was awake, the only thing that seemed to calm him was holding Robbie and me. He held us so tight that we could hardly breathe. Both of us boys knew he needed us, so we didn't care. As soon as he could get to a chair, we scrambled up onto his lap. Time after time he was so hot it felt like his body was going to catch on fire. Robbie and I almost always had to change our pj's because we were soaked from the sweat on his body. Kathy wrapped the three of us in clean, dry blankets and changed the sheets on the bed. I remember now that Kathy and Buddy had a plastic sheet on their bed just like some people used for little babies.

Kathy told me one time that Buddy was like Captain Moroni in the Book of Mormon. He would do anything that was necessary to keep us free. Even though the war had ended for most people, Buddy was still feeling the effects from what he had had to do to protect our freedom. She told me she never wanted me to take this country or our freedom for granted, and I never have.

One more experience will help you to get to know the kind of person Buddy is. I was in seventh grade and was playing basketball. Our team had only seven players, but we were so good we won almost every game we played. We went to Ridgeway to play in a tournament, and we made the finals. We had only one game to go to claim the championship. During lunchtime we went to the drugstore to get some pop, and while we were there, one of the boys dared me to take a pair of sunglasses. Like a stupid idiot, I took the dare. I had barely stepped out of the door when a big man grabbed me by the shoulder. I thought I was going to die! I thought of telling him that I had forgotten to pay for the sunglasses, but I knew I had better not add a lie to what I had done. He refused to let me pay for the sunglasses and had one of the boys go to get the coach. As you would expect, the coach was screaming mad. He took me by the arm and almost dragged me back to the school. The game was just about to start, and over the loudspeaker the announcer had just finished introducing the players on the other team and was announcing our team. When he came to my name, he announced that I would not be playing in the game because I had taken a pair of sunglasses from the drugstore and had not paid for them. Oh, how I wanted the floor to open up and swallow me! Having only 6 players in the second quarter, we had two players foul out. With only four players, our team was slaughtered. Our bus trip home must have been about a hundred miles, and my coach made me sit up front next to him so he could keep an eye on me. I don't think anyone said anything all the way home.

My weekend was a disaster! I stayed in my room, and Kathy was worried that I was sick. On Monday, when I got to my classroom, I was told that I had to go to the principal's office. Fear shot through me! I had heard stories about him having a huge paddle with lots of holes in it, and every time someone got a spanking, he would make them drill a hole in it before their swat. If you were slow in drilling the hole, he would swat you like a batter hitting a baseball, lifting you off the floor and setting you down several feet from where you had been standing. I heard that he even had marks on the floor so he could see if he could set a new record. When he opened the door, the first thing I saw was the drill, and then the paddle. Like a cat, I jumped all the way across the floor, grabbed the drill, and started drilling as fast as I could. I looked down, and sure enough, there were the marks on the floor. Apparently I drilled my hole fast enough because, when he hit me with the paddle, it stung like blazes, but at least he didn't throw me across the floor! I was relieved thinking it was all over, but it wasn't. The principal sat me down on the chair next to his desk and started talking to me about what I had done to my team, to the school, and to myself. The stinging was about to stop when he dropped the bomb. He told me that I could not come back to school until Buddy and I had gone to the owner of the drugstore and paid for the glasses. He also wanted a letter signed by the owner and Buddy saying that I had completed that task. I remember thinking, "Good Grief, will this thing never end?" I spent the next hour sitting in his office. I can't tell you all the thoughts that went through my mind, but in the end, I felt the best thing to do was to face the music.

When I got home from school, I told Kathy and Buddy what had happened. They never said a thing; they just sat there looking at me. I asked them if we could have prayers so I could go to bed, and that's what we did. Nothing was said about what I had done. Early the next morning we started the long trip to Ridgeway, and Buddy never said a word. Everything I had gone through, and this trip with Buddy refusing to talk to me, made a lasting impression on me. I was determined never to lie, steal, or disappoint him again.

By this time, Walker looked tired and asked me if we could take some time before he tells me more about Kathy. I agreed and asked him if he needed anything. "Thank you," he said in a weak voice. "I just need some rest."

CHAPTER 3

KATHY

Walker slept for a spell, and I sat and watched him sleep, pondering the reason why he needed to tell his story. When he woke, he was slightly disoriented, which prompted me to ask him if he was feeling okay. "Yes, I feel better now," he said. "What were we talking about?" Before I could answer, he said, "Oh yes. I was going to tell you about Kathy. She was wonderful." And he continued his narrative.

Kathy has an unbelievable history. Her father was a logger, and her mother was a homemaker. They had two children, a boy and a girl. The two were about all their mother could handle, as she wasn't in good health. Kathy's father worked out of town a lot as a logger, but he never sent money home while he was gone. Sometimes he was gone for months at a time. After her first two children were born, she apparently never planned to get pregnant again. Somehow it happened, and Kathy was born. Kathy's mother died when Kathy was about a year old. Someone told Kathy she believed her mother died from starvation because she had given all the food she had to her children. After Kathy's mother's death, her father turned the children over to the state. Kathy's sister was prone to having fits, so she was placed in a sanitarium where she received electric shock treatments. I met her once as an adult, and she seemed like a very nice person. I could see that she had had a real tough time because of the way her hands shook. Evidently, she shook so hard she had a difficult time dressing and feeding herself. Kathy said they had done some experiments on her brain and she was lucky to still be alive. I don't know if she had any quality of life, but she seemed happy when she was around Kathy.

Her brother, Steve, virtually became a slave. He was sent to foster homes where they needed cheap labor, and many times he was late for school because it took so long to finish his chores. When he arrived late to school, he had to hold out his hands with his palms up while his teacher swatted them as a consequence for being late. At twelve years of age, Steve was given a horrible beating by his foster father, and it took him several days to get back on his feet. When he was up to it, he ran away. The authorities caught him and sent him back to the same foster home, but as soon as he got a chance, he ran away again. His foster parents soon realized that they would have to beat him to death to keep him from running away, so they decided to let him go. He later joined the military, and when he got home, he looked up his real dad and found him almost broken and close to death. Even in this debilitating condition, he couldn't say a kind word to Steve. No matter how hard Steve tried to earn his father's love and approval, he received the worst treatment the man could dish out. Steve got to the point where he hated his father, God, and everyone else. He met his sister, Kathy, when she was fifteen years old, and from that time on, he worshipped the ground she walked on. Kathy was everything to Steve, and there wasn't anything he wouldn't do for her. Sometime later, Steve met a pretty lady who had had a stroke on her twenty-fifth birthday. She couldn't walk, talk, or remember much about her life. Her husband had divorced her and basically left her to die. I don't know anything about her family, but apparently they had abandoned her too. Steve took her under his wing and started taking care of her. During the next ten years, he was able to teach her to walk, talk, and take care of herself. Every time Kathy saw Steve, she suggested that he marry this lady, but he said he wouldn't marry her until she fully realized what she was doing. In time, they married, and Kathy said she had never seen Steve so happy.

Kathy tried to get Steve to join a church, but he hated God for all of the suffering he had gone through. The tough life he had led had affected his health, and he seemed to be going steadily downhill. Kathy was terribly worried about him. One day during a visit to Kathy's, Steve told her that he had found a Cowboy's Bible and had been reading it. He said that it was bringing him peace and comfort. He told her that he had forgiven his father and that he felt good that his wife could now care for herself. One night he died in his sleep, and Kathy said he was in a peaceful place now.

As a child, Kathy was moved around from home to home and was never able to stay in any one home for very long. Fortunately, most of the homes were very good ones. As she got older, the homes became more difficult to get along in, and luckily, she didn't have to stay in any home long enough for her existence to become unbearable. She was finally placed in a home she really loved where there were two baby boys and two slightly older girls. Kathy was allowed to care for them as if they were her own. She fell in love with them and they with her. She said that this was the happiest time of her childhood. One day the people from the state came and moved her. She later found out that the family had wanted to adopt her, but her father, who had never come to see her or any of his children for that matter, had refused to allow the adoption. Why he wouldn't let Kathy be adopted no one ever knew. She was moved to another home that had two girls about her age. The girls were very mean to her, but the parents let her go to church. The church showed a film on the life of Jesus, which affected her so deeply she became determined to develop a personal relationship with the Savior. She became so close to Him that she could actually talk to Him and He would answer her. I know this is hard to imagine, but you would have to know her to understand what I am telling you. She said it was a great comfort to her to know that Jesus would never let her down like her own father always had.

Kathy's next foster parents were the McCabes, who were an older couple who owned a farm.

Kathy was good at doing chores, and they had plenty to do on the farm. The only bad part was that the first week Kathy was there, Mr. McCabe caught her in the barn and forced her head into the milk cow station. He then proceeded to fondle her. This scared her to death because she had never been touched in that way before. She prayed fervently and a voice told her to tell him to stop because she was losing respect for him and she wanted to respect him and his wife. She did what the voice told her to do, and amazingly, he stopped and was a perfect gentleman from that time on.

The farm had large patches of blackberries during the summer, so Kathy always had enough to eat. She loved blackberries more than anything else she could think of. This home turned out to be the most stable home Kathy had been in. She was about college age by that time and was determined to go to college. She knew there was no money for her to go to college, so she figured she would get a job and pay for it on her own. Kathy made it through one semester, but she couldn't find a job for the next semester. Because she didn't know what to do, she called Mrs. McCabe, and Mrs. McCabe told her that she could always come home. That evening Kathy put out a "fleece" as Gideon had done in the Bible when he had wanted a sign from heaven concerning a decision he had to make. She told God that if it was raining in the morning, she would stay and keep looking for a job. If it wasn't raining, she would go home. The next morning it was raining and she had her sign. The very day she was to start her classes she was offered two jobs. One of the jobs was in a dairy, which gave her all the buttermilk and cheese she could eat, and the other job was on campus where she earned enough money to pay her tuition. Kathy graduated from college just like she had said she would.

All of her life Kathy lived by putting out fleeces to God, and she never doubted any answer she received. She had become a Nazarene when she attended Nazarene College, so when she started dating Buddy, who was a member of The Church of Jesus Christ of Latter-day Saints, she wasn't sure what she should do. She wondered whether she should date him, considering that they belonged to very different churches. Attending the Nazarene College had helped her to grow spiritually, but for some reason, she didn't feel fulfilled. Also, she had some serious questions about her religion. Buddy could see that Kathy was the most spiritual person he had ever met. There was only one problem; he would not marry outside his own church. Kathy agreed to take the missionary discussions and learn about Buddy's church, but Buddy was not taking any chances. He insisted on attending all the discussions with Kathy and the missionaries. Kathy loved the scriptures and had read the Bible from cover to cover five or six times. Every time she had a question about a scripture, she put a question mark beside it. She had discussed her questions with pastors from many different churches and most of the time was told that these were "God's mysteries" and she shouldn't be questioning them. When the missionaries started teaching her, she was almost beside herself because they were able to answer all of her questions. She couldn't wait to be baptized. Kathy and Buddy dated for a year after she was baptized, and then they were married in an LDS temple for all time and eternity.

Buddy and Kathy decided to start a family. The first pregnancy was really hard on Kathy, and she lost the baby boy a few days after he was born. That was a crushing blow, but what was even worse was the doctor telling her that another pregnancy would probably kill her. Kathy and Buddy simply wouldn't accept this. They were determined to try again, so they did. As a male member of The Church of Jesus Christ of Latter-day Saints, Buddy held the priesthood, so he was able to give Kathy a special husband's blessing when she got pregnant again. He was inspired to bless her that she would survive the pregnancy, but he received no inspiration regarding the welfare of the baby. All he knew was that the baby girl she was carrying was a very special spirit in the eyes of Heavenly Father. The pregnancy was so hard that Kathy spent almost the whole nine months in bed. Unfortunately, the baby girl died shortly after birth, and it took Kathy a long time to recover fully from the pregnancy and to regain her strength. Naturally, as soon as she regained her strength, they tried again, and within a short period of time she found out that she was pregnant. Once again Buddy blessed her that her life would be protected, but the inspiration didn't come to bless the baby that it would live. He received the knowledge that this baby, who was also a choice spirit, wanted to be born into a special family. He desired that Kathy and Buddy should be his parents, but he would only be here on the earth for a very short time. The couple was able to spend about two hours with their baby boy before he left them to return to his Heavenly Father. The pregnancy and birth had many complications, and Kathy's recovery this time was very slow. It took two years for Kathy to fully recover and then another year before Kathy conceived again. This pregnancy was much easier until the last month. Kathy's name was placed in the temple for a special blessing, and the members of the church fasted and prayed for her and the baby. Buddy and their bishop gave Kathy a blessing that she would be okay, but again, the baby wasn't mentioned. As they drove to the hospital, Kathy informed Buddy that she knew the baby wouldn't live. Kathy was right; their beautiful baby boy didn't live. Kathy told Buddy that, in her mind, she had seen two boys and a girl in their family, but Buddy said he didn't think he could go through another pregnancy. At that, they both laughed, knowing that Kathy was the one doing all the hard work. Kathy then took his face between both of her hands and kissed the top of his bald head. She didn't have to say anything because they both knew how hard that experience had been on both of them.

Sometime later, Buddy and Kathy fasted and prayed about once again trying to have another child. They both got the answer that a baby was coming. For two years, Kathy could not get pregnant.

Their faith was being sorely tried, but they didn't waiver. One Fast Sunday a visitor attended their church meeting. He said he had spent the night in Moab, Utah, and in the motel room next to him was a young Indian girl who had a baby boy. He said there were about five or six people staying in the room and they were all drunk. He knew the baby wasn't being taken care of properly, and he said he believed that if someone didn't do something, the baby wouldn't make it. Buddy and Kathy got the name of the motel, and the room number, and left immediately for Moab. It was getting fairly late when they arrived there, and sure enough, there was a big party going on in the motel room. Kathy stayed in the car while Buddy went into the room unannounced. No one seemed to care that he was even there because they were all in drunken stupors by that time. Buddy saw a little bundle in the corner of the room, and when he pulled the blanket back, he saw a baby with bulging eyes and sunken cheeks. It appeared that he hadn't been fed for some time and was in really bad shape. Also, it was obvious that the baby's diaper hadn't been changed for a very long time because the baby's legs and bottom were covered with sores. Without giving it a second thought, Buddy picked up the baby and headed for the door. One of the older men in the room stepped in front of Buddy and asked him what he thought he was doing and Buddy made it plain that he was taking the baby and going to the police. The man stepped aside and let him go. The Indian girl was totally out of it, but anyone could have figured out that she was most likely the baby's mother. As for the men, they knew they were in trouble.

Buddy and Kathy went straight to the authorities who proceeded to try to find a state worker to come and take the baby. While they were waiting, Buddy and Kathy decided to go to the store and get some diapers and medicine for the baby's sores. When the lady from the state came, she was amazed to see the baby all cleaned up. The police made a raid on the motel room and found it empty and there was no one around who knew where the room's occupants had gone. The room was a mess, but the police found some evidence that helped them find one of the men. It took a week for the police to find him, and when they did, the man couldn't give them any information about the baby's mother. That created a whole new problem concerning what to do with the baby who had been taken to the hospital because of the sores and dehydration as well as severe diarrhea. After a week in the hospital, he was ready to be released. Since Kathy had decided to stay with some members of the LDS church in Moab, she was given permission to help care for the baby who, by that time, had been placed in a temporary care home. Kathy busied herself helping the foster mother by changing the bandages on the baby's sores and comforting him.

Children's Services talked to Kathy about being a foster mother for the baby until his mother could be found. She already knew what Buddy's answer would be, so all that was left was filling out the paperwork and the baby boy would be ready to go home. The only problem was that the placement was going to be temporary and they were already head over heels in love with the little boy. Buddy and Kathy both knew it would be a crushing blow to them when the mother took him back. What was even worse, they felt the baby would not have a decent life with the mother, if he lived.

Then the dreaded day came; the mother was found. She was in an Albuquerque hospital and was in very bad shape. Buddy and Kathy spent a long time praying. Suddenly, Buddy got up and told Kathy he knew what to do. They got in the car and headed straight to Albuquerque. When they got there, Buddy went to the first lawyer's office he could find and made a simple request. First, he wanted papers drawn up giving full custody of the baby to him and Kathy. Then, he wanted adoption papers drawn up. At that point, they didn't even know what the baby's name was, so they left the name blank. They went to the hospital and found that the mother was just being moved out of intensive care and arrangements were being made to place her into a drug rehab facility. Buddy walked straight up to her and asked her to sign the custody papers.

Surprisingly, she signed them. Next, she signed the adoption papers. She told him that she had not given the baby a name because he had been born in a motel room. She signed a statement stating that the father was dead. Buddy and Kathy took the papers to the judge, and as amazing as it may sound, he signed the custody papers. Just like that, Kathy's vision of a little boy was fulfilled. Several years later, the adoption was granted. They named the baby boy Robbie, and he is the same boy I shared a room with when I went to live with Buddy and Kathy. Of course, he was older then. The adoption was a long, hard, and expensive process, but finally Robbie had not only a first name but a last name too.

Robbie's health wasn't good. He had some kind of spells, and when the spells happened, Kathy's life stopped. Every second of her time and every ounce of her energy were devoted to him. Buddy did all the chores, which totally freed Kathy up so she could care for little Robbie. And Robbie, as hard as he tried, just kept getting weaker, so he had a hard time doing normal things like playing sports. I felt kind of bad because everything always came easy for me. But even though Robbie had to struggle with most things, he never gave up. Kathy devoted a tremendous amount of time to his studies, and she did such a good job that no one ever knew about his handicap. As I said earlier, Robbie could read his little books very well at an early age.

I'm sure you've guessed by now that I could go on for days talking about those wonderful people who have blessed my life in so many ways.

I could see that telling these stories was very difficult for Walker and very taxing on his strength, so I suggested to him that he stop for the rest of the day and resume telling his story tomorrow. I figured a good night's sleep would help him regain his strength. "I know I don't have many tomorrows left," he said, "and my story has to be told. I'll only take a short break before I tell you about the most frightening experience of my childhood. I learned that one second can make or destroy a person's life." I watched as he closed his eyes and quickly fell asleep.

CHAPTER 4

EXTREME FEAR

I snared a rabbit while Walker was asleep, and I was cooking it when he woke up. "Rabbit! Did I tell you I used to hunt rabbits with Buddy?" he asked. I had let him sleep for several hours, and the oranges and pinks of the sunset were now brilliant on the horizon. Realizing how late in the day it was, Walker asked, "Why did you let me sleep so long? I don't have much time left, and I have so much to tell you! God has promised me that I will not leave until I can complete this journey with you." He refused to eat the rabbit I had cooked for him and continued his story.

I want to go back to the Bear Hunter incident. If you'll remember, he accused me of hurting his daughter, and my friends and I took quite a beating over the misunderstanding. He apologized and tried to make everything right when all I wanted to do was to have it all go away. Buddy had driven me home without saying anything, and it was an uncomfortable drive home. When we got there, I jumped out of the car and went in for lunch. Robbie and Kathy were already at the table waiting for prayers. Buddy almost always gave the blessing on the food, but this time he asked Kathy to do it, and as always, we had a very pleasant meal. You know, there is something wonderful about knowing that there is a safe time set aside where no matter what has happened during the day, only pleasant things will be discussed at the table. Unfortunately, the meal didn't last forever. While Kathy and Robbie cleared the dishes, Buddy went into the living room and sat down on the couch. He motioned for me to come and sit beside him. I asked him if we shouldn't be getting back to school, and he said, "We should, but first, you are going to tell me what you have done." Knowing I didn't have a choice, I told him that yesterday when

Kenny, Johnny, and I were walking home, we saw two boys pulling Bear Hunter's daughter's hair. They started throwing dirt and rocks at her and made her start crying. She kept it up and couldn't stop, so we told her we would walk her home. She didn't say she wanted us to take her home, but we decided to take her home anyway.

When we got to her house, we knocked on the door. Mrs. Hunter answered and asked what we wanted. Just then, her daughter ran past us into the house, still crying. Mrs. Hunter started yelling at us and telling us that we should leave her daughter alone. Then she slammed the door in our faces before we could even explain what had happened. We weren't sure what else we could do, so we just played some basketball and went home. The next morning, Bear Hunter called us out of class and took us upstairs to his office. We noticed that he had placed three chairs in front of his principal's chair, and we thought he was going to have us sit down so he could thank us for helping his daughter. Boy, were we surprised when he accused us of hurting her! He said we had cut some of her hair and that we had pulled her hair so hard that she had had a headache almost all night. He said that, because of us, she had refused to come back to school and even wanted to go back to Window Rock, Arizona, where the family used to live. He told us that Mrs. Hunter and their daughter had left for Window Rock that morning and weren't coming back. Bear Hunter asked us how we would feel if someone pulled our hair and threw rocks and dirt at us until we cried. Kenny yelled out, "We didn't do it!" and Bear Hunter grabbed him by the hair, shook him, and called him a liar. That's when I told him he was the liar, and he slapped me so hard it knocked me down. I screamed at him as loud as I could, saying, "You're the liar, not us!" and he started slapping me again. And that's when Johnny wet his pants. When I saw Johnny, I wet my pants too. I don't know why. I just did.

At that point, Buddy went to his room and came out with his rifle. He always used a 30–40 Krag, which is an awesome weapon that holds five bullets chambered from the side. I watched him flip the chamber open, and I could see it was fully loaded. He slammed the bolt closed and flipped the safety over while telling me to get into the car.

When we got to school, Buddy pulled the car into the opening used for the crosswalk and calmly stepped out of the car. He then got the rifle from the backseat. It was quite a distance to the building, but it seemed like it took us only seconds to get to the door. Buddy hit the door so forcefully that the doorjamb splintered, throwing the door wide open.

Bear Hunter was sitting at his desk when we got there, and I will never forget the look on his face when he saw Buddy with his 30–40 Krag. He knew he was in big trouble, so he rolled off the side of his chair and crawled under his desk. Buddy grabbed the desk with his free hand and flipped it over by the door like it was nothing. There was Bear Hunter on his knees with his hands clasped behind his head, as if his hands would protect his head from a bullet!

I was startled to see that Buddy's shirt had a sweat mark all the way down the middle of his back and his underarms were soaked clear down to his belt! I could actually feel the heat coming from his body just like when he had one of his nightmares. Fear shot through me because I knew that Bear Hunter was going to die! I stood there frozen to the floor. If anyone tells you things can go in slow motion, believe them. Everything seemed to have come to a complete stop. Buddy reached over to Bear Hunter, grabbed him by the collar of his shirt, and pulled his head back to where it touched the barrel of the gun. Buddy used his thumb to flip the safety off as his second finger moved from the trigger guard to the trigger. Native Americans tell about having their visions, and at that moment, I had mine. I could hear the deafening sound of the bullet and smell the smoke from the barrel of the gun. On the wall, I could see the splatter from the damage the bullet caused.

I became aware of Bear Hunter praying. Strangely enough, he wasn't praying for his own life but asking God to forgive Buddy for what he was going to do. He was telling God that he deserved what was coming to him because of the horrible things he had done to the little boys. Then he started chanting in his native tongue. Buddy's finger was still on the trigger and I had already seen what was going to happen.

As children, we learned not to get close to Buddy when he was having one of these spells. We knew it was safer to wait until he woke himself up. This time he was wide awake! I screamed in my mind, "God, please don't let this happen!" That very instant I felt something like a soft hand take me by my wrists. With one hand, I touched Buddy's cheek, and I told him it was all right, that he didn't need to do this. Buddy's skin was so hot I thought it was going to burn my hand. With my other hand, I reached across his hand and flipped the rifle back onto safety. Bear Hunter was continuing his chant while Buddy just stood there for what seemed like forever. Without saying another word, Buddy walked over to the desk and moved it so we could get out of the door. We walked back to the car, and only then did I realize that he had not turned the engine off. I noticed that he had stopped sweating and was once more in charge. I didn't say anything; I just went to my side of the car and climbed into the front seat. Buddy put the gun into the backseat, backed the car out, turned around, and went home. When we got to our house, Buddy took his gun and went into the bedroom where I could see Kathy still on her knees praying. He put the gun up, and they gave each other a long hug. As I think about it, I wonder if it was somehow Kathy's spirit that took me by the hands to defuse the situation. After that incident, Bear Hunter was a broken man. I don't know for sure, but I think his wife and daughter left him. He stayed at school until a replacement could be found. I never did hear anything more about him. It was funny because no one ever talked about what had happened.

"Walker, I can see you're in pain. Can I do anything for you?" I helped him shift his position, and I readjusted his blanket underneath him. "I might try a little soup if I can keep it down," he said. I took the meat from the rabbit and added it to the water I was boiling. A twinkle came into Walker's eyes. "I know what you're thinking, and yes, I always knew Buddy would do anything he had to do to protect his family from harm."

CHAPTER 5

MY GREATEST DISAPPOINTMENT

Most of the time, I didn't know what was going to happen each year when school was out. The day after school would end for the summer, Fat Man and either one or two ladies would show up at the house and spend several hours questioning Buddy and Kathy about me. I never forgot the first time they came to pick me up., Just seeing them caused me to have a panic attack.

I can remember the summer I turned eight years old. In our church, when children turn eight years old, they can be baptized if they have their parents' permission and the approval of their bishop. We had asked my aunt and uncle for permission for me to be baptized and were awaiting their decision. As usual, Fat Man showed up, but this time he didn't have the ladies with him. Instead, my aunt and uncle had accompanied him. When I saw them, I was so filled with anxiety and fear, I ran out of the room. This was unacceptable to Kathy. She told me that she had taught me better than that and there was no excuse for me not to be polite, so I went back into the living room and spent some time talking to my "family." They seemed to be very nice and told me that they loved me and wanted me to come home to live with them. They said they had two boys a little younger than I was and I would be a great older brother. Being well aware of how families are when they have their own children, I told them in the politest way possible that I had a younger brother and we depended on each other. I could never go anywhere without him because he would never leave Kathy and Buddy, so I would have to stay there. I asked them why they thought I would ever want to leave, and their answer was simple, "We are your family, and we love you."

I asked them how I could make them understand that Buddy and Kathy were the only family I had ever known and that Kathy, Buddy, and Robbie needed me and could never be happy without me. And I could never be happy without them! How could they ask me to disappoint my family, my brother, my team, my teacher, and my church friends? What about my paper route and all the people whose yards I was taking care of? Didn't they know those people depended on me? What would they all do without me? Didn't they know that all these people loved me too? I told them that if they really loved me, they would leave me alone! I asked them to please tell me what I needed to do to make them go away and never come back.

My aunt was crying, and my uncle was staring at the floor. They were both silent for a long time. I wanted to say more, but I heard a whisper in my mind saying, "Don't say another word." Everyone in the room, except for the two lawyers, got up and quietly left the room. I didn't want to talk to them, but I had to ask them what right they had to do this to us. I told them that this was my family and my life, and I asked them to please go away. My uncle's lawyer told me that he had every right to do this and he also had the power to take me with him or to leave me here with these people. I looked into his eyes and I knew that he was telling the truth. I was scared of this man because he seemed to be a man with no heart. Buddy's lawyer said, "That's enough," and told me I could leave the room.

Buddy and Kathy went into the living room to meet with the lawyers, and it seemed like they were in there for a long time. My aunt and uncle had stayed in their car. It was hot in the house but even hotter in the car. I looked at them and my first thought was, "I hope you roast in that car and are so miserable that you never come back!" But then, Kathy's teachings came into my mind. Knowing what she would say, I went to the fridge, got a pitcher of water with ice, and filled six glasses. When I took some water into Buddy, Kathy, and the two lawyers, I could tell things weren't going well. Then I took a pitcher of water out to the car. My aunt and uncle asked me if I would like to stay and talk to them, but I could see no good reason to stay, so I politely refused and walked back into the house.

My aunt and uncle's lawyer wouldn't give an inch. He decided he would let me stay for the time being, but with one stipulation. I was not to be baptized. I was developing a bad history with these people.

When I was ten years old, I had a better understanding about what was going on. School was out, and once again, Fat Man and the lawyers were on our doorstep. This time, they had more reasons for being there. The issues were again my baptism and my being adopted. Robbie was turning eight years old and was going to be baptized, and Kathy and Buddy wanted me to be baptized with him if it was at all possible. I wanted it so badly my heart was pounding! I realized that this time they wanted to take me back to the reservation because I had family there who wanted me to live with them. I didn't know it before, but evidently my aunt and uncle were leaders on the reservation who had a lot of authority. Fat Man and the lawyers took me to a room and asked me a lot of questions about my school, etc. My grades were the best in my class, and I was the best player in all the sports I was participating in. I had done my paper route all these years and hadn't had any complaints. I also took care of a large number of yards while people went on vacation. In other words, I had my own money and bought my own school clothes. I would always buy Robbie what I bought for myself. I had my own gun, bow and arrows, all the fishing gear a person could want or need, my own sports equipment, and my own lawn mower and yard equipment. In addition, I attended church every week.

It did not go well. My aunt and uncle didn't show up that year, but they sent the lawyer without a heart to represent them. Our requests were all turned down, and he made it very clear to Buddy and Kathy that they were not my parents and had very few rights in this case. When I heard that, I exploded and started screaming that they were my parents. I went up to the lawyer and screamed in his face, "they are my mom and dad!' Buddy grabbed me by the arm and took me outside. I ran to the living room window and kept screaming and pounding on the window, "They are my mom and dad!" I was screaming so loud that the neighbors all came out to find out what was going on. I kept it up until I lost my voice. I needed to do something to stop those people! From that day on, I never again called them Kathy and Buddy. They are, and always have been, Mom and Dad, and I don't know why I ever started calling them Kathy and Buddy in the first place. When Fat Man and my uncle's lawyer left, I was so furious that I threw a rock at their car and busted out the back window. That created a major firestorm, which took another couple of hours to resolve. By that time, I was filled with hate, and I knew that someday, one way or another, I was going to put a stop to this. After the others left, our lawyer stayed to talk to Kathy and Buddy. I couldn't hear all of what was said, but I did hear that they were telling him to do all he could regarding the adoption. He replied that this was getting to be very expensive and they were up against the tribe who seemed to be willing to use all their resources to get their way. Buddy said he had a buyer for one of his mines and that he was going to sell it, so the lawyer could go ahead with our case. He said that my aunt and uncle might love me, but he knew, as God was his witness, that he and Kathy loved me more.

That evening we had a family council, which was not our usual council because it was so solemn. Robbie was going to be turning eight in the near future, and it would be time for him to be baptized. Kathy and Buddy had done all they could do to get permission from my aunt and uncle for me to be baptized with Robbie, but to no avail. They said that when I turned twenty-one, no one could stop me from being baptized. Our bishop came by to talk to me, and he took me into a room so he could talk to me alone. We had a long talk about Heavenly Father and how He is just and fair with everyone. He said that there were times when someone else makes it impossible for us to do what we need to do to obey Heavenly Father, and when this happens, the people involved will have to pay for what they've done. He told me I needed to have faith in His justice and that He was aware of what was happening to me. He said everything that had been said and done was being recorded, and if the tribe's lawyer and his people needed to be punished, it was up to God to do it. He told me that no matter what, I shouldn't hate them, and I knew what he said was true. He told me that if I desired to be baptized and someone forcibly kept me from doing it, in Heavenly Father's eyes, it was already done and the Savior would take care of the details. He told me what Mom and Dad had told me, "When you turn twenty-one, you can be baptized and no one can stop you."

Robbie said he wanted to put off his baptism until I turned twenty-one. That sounded great, but it didn't help much. I really wanted and needed to be baptized now. I told Robbie how much I loved him and how I could not stand the idea of him not being baptized. I asked him to please go ahead so I could take part in it. Robbie asked me if I would give the opening prayer, and I told him I would be glad to.

My heart was crushed, but then I had a brilliant idea. I knew that God can do anything. So that evening I got on my knees and told God that I would always be good and never sin again if He would make my aunt and uncle change their minds. It was three months before Robbie's eighth birthday, and I knew there would be plenty of time for God to work everything out so I could be baptized with Robbie. I could relax now. As the weeks passed, the excitement increased. We had relatives coming from everywhere, and I wanted my prayer to be answered soon so I could get going with my plans.

We finally came to the morning of the baptism. I woke up early, and the thought came to my mind that this was Robbie's day, not mine. I was being very selfish. I got out of bed and got down on my knees calling upon God, the Creator of the heavens and the earth, the One who can do anything, to ask Him to rescind my request. I told Him that if it was His will, I was willing to wait until I turned twenty-one to be baptized. It was like a massive weight was lifted off my shoulders. Now I could really get into this day and enjoy it with Robbie.

In our church, baptism is a very formal and sacred ordinance. Baptism can only be performed by those who have the priesthood authority to baptize. Buddy, who was going to perform Robbie's baptism, was able to trace his priesthood authority all the way back to Joseph Smith, who received his priesthood authority from the resurrected Peter, James, and John. Peter, James, and John received their priesthood authority directly from Jesus Christ who received his authority from his Heavenly Father. All male members of The Church of Jesus Christ of Latter-day Saints have the opportunity to receive the priesthood. One of the greatest honors and privileges in the church is for fathers to be able to baptize their own children and other family members as well as close friends who have requested it. Since baptism requires the permission of a child's parents or legal guardian, I was not able to be baptized.

The baptism ceremony was going beautifully because Mom always set everything up perfectly. My uncle Glenn, Buddy's brother, was giving a talk on baptism, and every time I looked at Mom, she started crying. I knew it was because of me, so I went over to her and pulled her beautiful hair away from her ear and whispered, "I know that I am ruining this for you. I will go into the hall and sit there until the ceremony is over." She put her arm around my waist and pulled me over to her. She lowered her head to where her hair covered my face and pressed her head as close to mine as possible. Even so, I didn't move. I needed her, and I had the feeling that she needed me too. Then I heard the gentle, but powerful, sound of Dad's voice as he said, "Robbie Lee Smith, having been commissioned of Jesus Christ, I baptize you in the name of the Father, and of the Son, and of the Holy Ghost, Amen." As Robbie went down into the water, I felt like I was drowning in Mom's hair. Then I could hear Robbie come up out of the water. At the same time Mom loosened her grip on me, and in a way, it was like I was coming up out of the water myself! I can tell you with all of my heart that what the bishop told me was true. I felt that Jesus had accepted me as if had been baptized too.

"These memories are very painful for me so I don't want to talk about it anymore," said Walker. "Can we please call it a night and start again in the morning?" Walker looked ancient and withered from the experience of relating his story. Our campfire was beginning to dim, and my eyes were wet with tears. I told him that I needed to stop also. "Thank you," he said as he drifted off to sleep. I sat looking into the sky full of stars and thanked Heavenly Father for guiding me to Walker.

CHAPTER 6

THE MESA

A trail of smoke drifted lazily from our campfire as the light of a new day slowly filled the sky. Walker was awake before me, though he didn't have the strength to move. He asked for help to sit up. His illness hung on him, drawing him to the ground for his final rest. I was surprised when he refused breakfast insisting that we continue. I had barely retrieved my pencil and paper when he began.

Do you want to know what a great life is? A great life is having Buddy and Kathy for parents, Robbie as a brother, and a great sports season to top it off. I've told you I delivered papers, had lawns to mow during the summer, and was able to buy my own clothing but I was also able to buy Buddy, Kathy, and Robbie almost anything I wanted to get them. I was getting older, and I excelled in everything I did. It was like I could do anything with almost no effort at all. My only real worry was Robbie.

Robbie was getting weaker, and even though he was doing great in school, he had to put in a tremendous effort. Thank God for Kathy who spared no effort in working with him! Sometimes I would wake up late at night, and those two would be hammering out some concept that Robbie was struggling with in school. They didn't stop until he got it. There were times when they worked all night with no sleep, and Robbie still went to school the next day. Kathy waited outside Robbie's classroom door for school to let out. The teacher knew she would be there, so she graded Robbie's papers as soon as he handed them in. Most often he got B's, but sometimes he would get an A. An A meant it was time for celebrating, and believe me, we celebrated! It always seemed that neither Robbie nor Kathy noticed that they had missed a night's sleep.

Walker paused and a broad smile crossed his lips. "I changed my name when I was twelve."

He watched me, waiting for my response.

"Did you add Smith to your name?"

"No, I always called myself Windwalker Smith. That year, I started to go by Walker."

"Why did you change it?" I asked.

"Well, it's kind of childish. Perhaps I shouldn't bring it up."

I could see his eyes dance, begging me to ask him more about it. "If you don't mind relating the story, I would like to know," I said.

I was in class with one of my cousins, Buddy, who sat next to me. Please excuse me for saying this, but he was famous for being able to fart anytime he wanted to. One day in class while we were saying prayers, he fired off like a foghorn. My eyes were closed, but I could hear everyone around me moving. When I opened my eyes, I was sitting at my desk, and everyone else, including Buddy, was standing up against the walls. Everyone pointed to me and said, "Windy did it!"

The next day, during a basketball game, I jumped to make a basket, and Buddy fired off again. Both my team and the other team pointed to me. "Windy did it!" I don't think the crowd could hear, but with nine other boys holding their noses and pointing to me saying, "Windy did it!" I'm sure they got the general idea about what had happened. The teasing got so bad I had to talk to Mom and Dad about it. After all, Buddy was my cousin! My dad and my uncle Glenn took Buddy into a room by himself and talked to him for a long time. I don't know for sure, but I believe he gave them a demonstration or two. When he came out, he said he was sorry and that he would never embarrass me like that again. Now all I had to worry about was the rest of the kids! Mom's solution was simple: change my name to Walker Smith and let the "Windy" part rest for a while. It worked!

With the name change, you could say my life was just about as good as it gets.

When I was thirteen, a young couple in their early thirties moved into our neighborhood, and I saw a chance to get another newspaper customer. When I went up to their door, I met Bart Durham who appeared to be Roy Rogers, Rex Ritter, and the Lone Ranger all rolled into one. From that moment on he was my idol. His wife, Bobbie, was not only good looking but also one of the kindest, sweetest, and most wonderful people I had ever known.

Bart handed me an atlatl and asked me if I knew how to use one. I told Bart that not only had I not used one but I also had no idea what it even was. He asked me if I had a bow and arrows. Of course I did! He said that if I loved my bow, I would really love the atlatl. It had darts that went with it, which were like little spears. He told me this was the weapon the ancient people used when they hunted the woolly mammoth. They could bring it down with this spear thrower, which is a very powerful weapon and a whole lot of fun.

The next things he unpacked were his guns. What an assortment! He had a holster for quick draw. He also had a holster with two pistols that had ivory grips, which he kept in a sealed case. He told me the story that went with them, but I didn't know who or what he was talking about.

Let's get back to the quick draw. The holster didn't have the barrel of the pistol go down the thigh like the ones you see in the movies. His was on his belt and lay across his waist with the gun barrel maybe two inches below the belt line instead of up and down on his leg. So if he was standing sideways to you, the barrel would be pointing at you while still in the holster. He handed me a cap pistol and told me he could draw and shoot before I could even pull the trigger. And to my amazement, he could! He would stand sideways with the barrel of the gun pointing toward me while still in the holster. When he proceeded to draw his pistol out, he only had to move the gun a few inches. The hammer was cocked as he pulled the gun out of the holster. I couldn't pull the trigger on the cap gun before he was able to draw and shoot! When it came to fanning, or shooting six shots as fast as you can, he had his own way of doing it. In the movies, they used their open left hand and moved it back and forth over the hammer as fast as possible. Bart spread his fingers apart using one finger to cock the gun with the trigger pulled back, so when his finger slipped off the hammer, the gun fired. He did the same with each of his fingers until he had fired five shots in about one second. The shots were so close together they almost sounded like one shot. He always left one bullet in the chamber so he would never have an empty gun.

We went into the back bedroom, and I noticed there were shelves covering the walls, which I assumed were bookshelves. The room was stacked with boxes, and Bart asked me if I would like to help him unload the boxes. I would have liked to help out, but I had already been there for quite a while and needed to get my papers delivered. He said he could use some help tomorrow, but darn it, I had baseball practice tomorrow. So we left the time open.

I loved books and couldn't wait to see what he had. It seemed like forever before I got back there.

When I walked into the bedroom, my mouth dropped to the floor. The shelves were filled with wooden dolls, and they all had feathers, beads, and clothing made for them! They were beautifully colored, and the display was very impressive. I told Bobbie that she must really like dolls, and to my surprise, she told me they belonged to Bart. I would never have imagined him playing with dolls!

When Bart got home, he took me into the room and gave me one of the greatest history lessons anyone could ever get. His lesson was all about the history of the Native American people living in the Four Corners area. The dolls were Katcina dolls carved by the Hopi Indians for use in their ceremonies, and Bart was one of the few white people allowed to attend these ceremonies. Because he was an artist, he drew pictures of their ceremonial costumes, which were visual records of the meanings of the ceremonies. The Hopis were concerned that they were starting to lose their traditions. Since all of their traditions were oral, and many of their young people were no longer following the ancient ways, they were grateful for Bart's drawings and writings, which helped to preserve their traditions. I spent every minute I could with him, and I think I now know more about the Native American people than most of the people on the reservation!

Bart and Bobbie spent as much time as possible scouring the surrounding area for Indian relics, and they had an arrowhead and spear point collection second to none. Every time they went relic hunting, they asked me to go with them. Mom and Dad had one basic rule. If I had my work done, the rest of the day was mine and I could do as I wished, as long as they knew where I was. And heaven help me if I was supposed to be somewhere and didn't go where I said I was going. Bart and Bobbie were great motivators for me to get my work done because I never knew when they would be going on one of their relic-hunting expeditions.

Sometimes Robbie came along with us to listen to the stories Bart told about the Indians, but when we went to the mountains, he stayed home. He knew he couldn't keep up with us, and he didn't want to hold us back. Bart, Bobbie, and I never felt good about leaving him home, but we never did embarrass him by insisting that he come along.

Some of the men in Uravan had gotten together and bought an airplane and they decided to use the level area on the north side of the canyon where we lived as a landing strip. The problem was that the landing strip was a favorite home for prairie dogs, and their holes were very dangerous for the plane. The men paid me five dollars and gave me all the shells I needed to shoot the destructive little varmints. Bart helped me sometimes when he and Bobbie weren't hunting for relics. We had two favorite ways of hunting the prairie dogs. When we first arrived, we would walk through the prairie dog town with our bows and shoot as many as we could. We kept score to see which one of us could get two with the same arrow. If one of us got three with one arrow, he got the entire dessert Bobbie had fixed for us.

After we made the trip with our bows, we set up in one of the airplane hangars and used our rifles to see how many more we could pick off. After about an hour, we filled in as many prairie dog holes as we could and went back to the car where Bobbie was waiting for us. Even though she liked to shoot, and would wait for us to finish our chore, she had decided early on that she would not shoot the cute little critters. We spent the rest of the day in the surrounding hills looking for the tallest sagebrush, which was where we were able to find most of our arrowheads, beads, pottery, and other interesting stuff. Bobbie told me that these were the areas where the Indians usually buried their dead. Bart took great pains to document everything we found. He was a great artist, and when he was through, you could look at his drawings and see what was found and exactly where it was found. Most of the time we put everything back the way we found it. The day's work was so hard I usually fell asleep in the car on the way home.

One Saturday at about 5:00 a.m., Bart woke me up by knocking on my window. He was all excited because he and Bobbie had found the "treasure of all treasures." He asked me if I wanted to go, and I jumped at the chance. I woke up Mom and asked her if I could go. Robbie followed me into Mom's room and told her that he would do my chores if she would please let me go. She reluctantly agreed, and I was out of there. I grabbed my clothes and ran out to the car. Bart and Bobbie had found three flattop mesas down in a deep canyon. The only way to get up onto a mesa was by climbing up the narrow crevasses. Only one person could climb up at a time, which made the mesa very defensible. When we reached the top, we could see that the area had been used as a refuge by the people who had lived there hundreds, or even thousands, of years ago to protect themselves from raiders. On top of each mesa was an area where the sandstone had been scraped out to trap rainwater. The water was cold and clear and deep. As we looked around, we could see that there were a lot of edible plants on the mesa. Bart said the Indians had probably planted them so that they would have food to eat when they went up there. Over the years, the plants just kept on reseeding and growing. On each mesa, rocks had been stacked up so that pack rats would build nests and store food there that the people could eat. We found the huge nests filled with pinion nuts and other kinds of food. All three mesas were basically set up the same way, so a fairly large group of people could live there for quite a long time. They had complete safety there. Bart was right; he had found the greatest treasure I had ever seen in my young life. We spent almost the whole summer up there, and each time we went up there, we found something even more exciting. Our greatest find was the honey trap. The Indians had set up large stones against a wall and apparently planted a honey bee colony. At the bottom of the rock, we could see where they had built fires to heat the rock, which caused the honey to flow out of the crack into a little basin where it could be gathered into clay pots. We even found some of the cedar posts they might have used for firewood. I regularly found myself wondering how many people had lived there and for how long. How many years ago had they cut those posts? We built a fire and took home about three gallons of the best honey I have ever tasted. We found another area where there were large stones stacked up in a pile, and we wondered what they were used for. After the first month on the mesas we discovered the answer. It was a deer trap. Rocks were strategically placed along a narrow gorge where deer passed through as a shortcut so they wouldn't have to go around the mesa. The stone piles created an area that was so narrow only one deer could go through at a time. When a deer had been singled out, the Indians on top of the mesa would throw large stones and kill the deer. What a clever and easy way to save their arrows and get their fresh meat!

As we sat at the edge of the cliff, Bart and I were amazed at the different wildlife we could see from the top of the mesa. Bart spent hours talking about the Indians who had lived in the area. I was becoming aware of my great heritage and beginning to fall in love with the Hopi culture. I was beginning to see why my aunt and uncle wanted me to go with them; they wanted me to remain close to our traditions. Bart said that the old ways were disappearing and many of the young people were disoriented by all the government handouts. This was one of the leading causes of the alcohol and drug abuse among the Indian nations. Every time he talked about it, I could hear the sadness in his voice. It left me wondering how a person like Bart could fall so much in love with a people that were not his own. I guess the Hopi people were his own, in a way, because of the work he was doing with them. I loved looking at his drawings because he had a way of bringing them to life. He was working on one that had mine and Robbie's faces on it. I think he was preparing it just for us.

One afternoon, when I got home from delivering my papers and mowing three lawns, Bart's car was parked in front of the house. Bart was there talking to Mom and Dad, and I don't know why, but when I glanced at Mom, I thought for a moment that I saw tears in her eyes. I was so glad to see Bart, and then I noticed that he was sitting next to my camping gear. To my surprise, we were going camping for the next five days. The trip was going to include Sunday. My family had never missed church, even when hunting and fishing. No matter where we were, we would go home to attend church and then go back to where we had been. Robbie was going to take care of all my work while I was gone. I don't know why, but he loved to take over my jobs. Perhaps it made him feel more like a normal kid. Whatever the reason, it was a blessing to me because it freed me up to do a lot of things that I normally wouldn't have been able to do.

There is a little creek called Spring Creek that was on the way to the mesas. We stopped there and loaded up on little brook trout. We built a fire, and when we caught three or four fish, we cleaned them and filled the insides with butter and onions before wrapping them in foil and dropping them onto the coals. We ate them almost as fast as we could catch them. If you haven't eaten fish prepared like that, you really need to try it; it's great! After we stuffed ourselves, we headed for the mesas.

Bart took me to a place he had been working on for several weeks in preparation for trapping rabbits. He had found an outcropping of rocks where a lot of rabbits were living. On one of the main rabbit trails, he had cut some sagebrush and made a kind of channel that the rabbits would have to go through to get to their holes in the rocks. We watched and waited for the rabbits to come out and forage for food. After a good number of rabbits had moved beyond the sagebrush channel, we put a gunnysack in the opening so we could chase the rabbits into our sack. We went about fifty yards from the outcropping of rocks and started running back and forth making as much noise as we could. We scared up a few cottontails and one big jackrabbit, but when they hit the sack, they tore it loose from the sagebrush it was tied to. One of the little cottontails escaped, but we got there in time to close the sack on the other two and the big jack. This was the great thing about my relationship with Bart; he was always teaching me survival techniques.

We made a cage of sticks in which to keep the jack and had the two cottontails for supper. I wasn't sure why we didn't turn the jack loose. I knew better than to ask Bart what we were going to do because he never explained his intentions beforehand. He would only tell me I needed to learn to be patient and that I would learn more that way. Staring at that jack, I knew I was in for some great learning experiences! I couldn't sleep because of the anticipation of what tomorrow would bring.

I was up early and had breakfast ready before Bart woke up. We wolfed down our food and tied a pole on the rabbit cage so we could carry it on our shoulders. Since I was quite a bit shorter than Bart, the weight was pushing down on me, which made it quite uncomfortable. The cage swung back and forth, and the jack slammed against the sides of it, making it hard to walk. In addition to that, Bart made me carry water. He said we had a long way to go.

After several hours, we reached our destination, which was a much smaller mesa than the three we usually explored. As we climbed up through the crevasse to the top, I couldn't help wondering why we needed the jack. When we got to the top of the mesa, I could see this mesa was different from the other two. The back side sloped down to the level ground, and it didn't give the same fortified protection as the others. Bart pointed out a large tree on the side of a nearby hill that had a huge nest of sticks in it. He told me the nest was an eagle's nest, which had probably been used for a hundred years or more. At the edge of the cliff was another rock outcropping where there were lots of rabbits. Bart said that was a favorite hunting area for the eagle family that lived in the nest. Then he told me he was going to help me get my first eagle feather.

I could hardly believe it! I wondered how someone could get an eagle feather without a rifle or a bow. Wasn't it illegal to shoot eagles? I noticed that a bunch of sagebrush had been cut and stacked in such a way as to provide a hiding place. Bart had apparently made this blind some time ago. He said he had spent several weeks tying rabbits next to the shelter so the eagles could get them. He explained that the eagles were used to getting the bait and would come at the first sound of the rabbit's distress. By bringing the jack into the makeshift cage, he was already agitated, which increased his appeal to the eagle family. We crawled into the blind. Bart took the jackrabbit, tied his hind leg, and put him in the same place he had put the others. Immediately, the jack gave out a bloodcurdling squeal. The more it fought the rope, the more it squealed. Bart told me that when the eagle latched on to the rabbit, it would hold on and he would have a chance to grab the eagle's legs. Bart had brought some heavy gloves for that purpose. My job was to put a hood over the eagle's head while Bart was holding its legs. The eagle would then calm down so we could get a tail feather. It sounded so simple. Little did I know!

We saw the eagle's shadow as it headed for the jackrabbit. When it hit, we could hear the crunching of bones as its powerful talons sank deep into the rabbit's flesh. Unlike the other rabbits this one was tied down so the eagle couldn't lift off with it. Like a shot, Bart left the blind and dove for the eagle's legs and clamped on. Then the war began! The bird was powerful and had the means to defend itself. He used his wings like weapons, throwing Bart around like a rag doll. I couldn't get to the bird's head to put the hood on, and the longer it took, the more vicious the great bird became! One of its talons came loose from the rabbit and caught Bart's forearm, ripping the flesh wide open to the bone. I was horrified as I watched the bird forcing Bart toward the edge of the cliff!

I made three or four desperate dives for the head of the eagle and finally, somehow got the hood over it, but he didn't stop thrashing around like Bart had said he would! Bart hung on anyway.

I kept working with the hood until I got it tight around his head. Soon, the eagle started to calm down, and in a short time, he was quite docile. Bart told me to take my belt and put it around his wings. We had caught an eagle!

I couldn't believe how heavy and how powerful the great bird was. He had thrown Bart around as if he was a rag doll. But now I couldn't believe how calm he had become. The bird was still holding on to the jack with one of his powerful talons. Bart told me to take a feather from the middle of the tail, but pulling the feather out was almost as difficult as catching the bird! After a short struggle, I finally got it to come out. To my surprise, I could see blood where I had pulled out the feather. Then Bart told me to go to the breast of this great bird and pull out some of the lighter-colored down feathers. I wasn't sure I wanted to get in front of it where its beak was, but with the hood over its head, it still remained calm. I took enough feathers to satisfy Bart.

I had sweat and dirt in my eyes, and Bart had blood mixed with sweat and dirt all over his face. We took a minute to admire that wonderful creature. I was even able to pet it like someone would pet a dog or cat. Everything became calm; it was like we were in a different world.

I took my prize feather and put it in a safe place. Then Bart told me it was time to release the eagle. He had hung a rope from the branch of a tree, and we put the eagle down and tied the rope to the hood. I loosened the knot on the hood and Bart told me to pull the hood off when he unbuckled the belt. As I pulled the hood off, the eagle just sat there and looked at us. Somehow, I had the feeling he was admiring us for what we had done. After what seemed like a long time, he opened his wings as if he were stretching. He then lifted off, still holding on to his rabbit, and flew toward the nest.

Bart's arm was still bleeding badly, so he went to the blind he had made to retrieve a first-aid kit. We filled the ugly-looking wound with disinfectant and made some butterfly bandages to dress the wound. It took quite a while to finally get the bleeding stopped. I suddenly realized what we had done and started shaking uncontrollably. I had my feather, the greatest gift Bart could ever have given me! As God is my witness, there is no man I admire and respect more than Bart. I have never in my life known another man like him!

I told Walker that God must have had a hand in putting Bart in his life. He said that God had more in store for him on that trip, but he couldn't go on anymore. I could see he was quite pale and very weak. I told him I would prepare something for us to eat and then we would both rest. But I didn't feel like eating. I just wanted to know what was coming next.

CHAPTER 7

THE ANCIENT ONES

Walker rested while I made some lunch, and it was all I could do to let him rest. The story of the eagle was thrilling and left me wanting more. I fixed a broth from some jerky I'd brought, and after a short while, Walker was ready to continue. Since the sun was working its way up into the sky, I took the time to clean up the lean-to shelter in which Walker had been living on the mesa. When he continued, I was ready.

I was walking on air all the way back to our mesa, but by the time we got to our camp, the adrenaline was wearing off. Bart's dressing was beginning to leak, and he was in quite a bit of pain. We were only beginning to discover how badly he was hurt. We changed the dressing and tried to stitch up the wound with butterfly bandages but couldn't get them to hold. The sight of the horrible wound made me sick, and I threw up. After my stomach settled a bit, I prepared our meal of pork and beans, sliced carrots dipped in honey, and a big pot of hot chocolate to top off our extraordinary day. As the sun dipped behind the hill, it became quite cold. I went a little way from camp to have my prayers, but when I returned, Bart told me he didn't mind if I prayed with him. Strange, I never thought of Bart as a praying man. We decided we would start blessing our food together instead of me quickly blessing the food under my breath. Not having slept very well the night before, and having had a very active day, the ground seemed softer than I remembered. I don't think I moved all night!

The next morning was Sunday. When I woke up, it was just starting to become daylight and Bart was sitting on the edge of the cliff with one leg dangling over the edge. He motioned to me to come and sit beside him and told me he was going to show me something that most people never see. He pointed out that, even though there was some light, everything was gray and lacking color. He said that if I sat still and watched closely, in the blink of an eye, there would be a moment when everything would take on color. After sitting there for about ten minutes gazing at the grays and blacks of the early dawn, to my amazement, I blinked my eyes and suddenly I was able to see the green of the trees and plants and the red of the sandstone all around us. As I looked down, I could see the valley below, and I got this real strange feeling in my stomach. It was then that I realized I had a fear of heights!

Bart said he had promised Mom that on Sunday we would not do any fishing, hunting, or hiking and that we would use this as a day of rest and worship. Sitting there at the edge of the cliff looking at the valley below us was one of the most peaceful experiences I've ever had. I turned to share it with Bart, but got the feeling that his mind was off in deep thought, as if he had forgotten I was even there. We watched silently as the world woke up around us.

The breeze on the back of my neck was giving me a chill, and I was getting hungry, so I decided I would go start breakfast. We had brought some bacon and eggs, which we had put into burlap sacks and soaked in water from the ancient cistern. We kept the burlap sacks wet all the time, and as I retrieved the sack and reached into it, I was surprised at how cold the bacon was. It was still as cold as it was when I had taken it out of the refrigerator.

When we were in the mountains, Bart always insisted that I start a fire by either rubbing sticks together or by using a flint stone. That day I decided to use the flint stone because it was the Sabbath and I didn't want to work too hard out of respect for God. I had my dry tinder ready, and it amazed me how quickly the fire started. The first thing I did was cook the bacon, and then I used the grease from the bacon to cook the eggs. By the time the eggs were done, Bart had left the edge of the cliff and was standing there with his plate in his hand. On that cool, clear morning, the grease on the bacon and eggs turned hard and stuck to the roof of our mouths. It was a tremendous breakfast, and a tremendous morning!

After we finished breakfast, we returned to the edge of the mesa. I asked Bart if he could tell me about the people who used to live there. Bart said that the pottery and basket remnants he had found indicated that they were farmers who had not only raised food but also had stored it up on the mesa. He believed there might have been raiders in the area and the people had to go up there for protection. He asked me if I noticed all the pools of water on the mesas. I had, but I hadn't given it much thought. All I knew was that I loved to drink the cool, clear water after the long, hard climb getting up onto the mesas. He told me that the people who used to live up there dug holes out of the soft sandstone to trap the rainwater. As I looked, I could see hand-dug trenches running from smaller water traps to a larger cistern dug at the base of the sandstone slope. With water, they could live up there quite a while when there were raiders down below. He said that place was the best natural fort he had ever seen. Since only one person could climb up through the crevasses at a time, a small number of people could hold off a whole army. He told me to go over to the edge of the mesa because he wanted to show me something. I was uncomfortable about getting that close to the edge! He pointed out that there were places where the trees had apparently been cleared for the planting of crops and explained how they were staggered intentionally. He said that when the raiders entered the area, the farmers would sound a warning and the workers would quickly fall back into the trees and disappear. I could picture how the workers followed the tree lines back to the mesa without ever being seen. He also pointed out that no one could come within nineteen miles without being detected. The mesa is where all the food was located, so the raiding parties gained little in that area. He told me he believed that the people who had lived there led a peaceful and abundant life. The way they planned their community and crops spoke to their intelligence and knowhow as stewards of the earth, not only in feeding themselves, but in protecting themselves as well. Throughout my early years, I'd heard that the Indians who lived in this area were backward and nothing but barbarians. Mom and Dad taught me that they were wise and industrious people. From Bart and my experience on the mesas, I saw how intelligent those people had to have been. As we sat on the edge of the cliff, Bart educated me on the people who had lived there, telling me who they were and how they had lived. I loved hearing his stories!

As Bart entertained, he questioned me to see what I knew about the Hopis, where they came from, how they lived, and where they live now. I was aware of them because Dad had a couple of mines on reservation land. When he and I inspected the mines, we usually stayed with some of the families who worked in his mine. We'd even had the opportunity to watch some of the Hopi ceremonies. Bart said the Hopis live in the oldest, continuously inhabited villages in the United States. They call their cities "the cities that are set up on the hill," and the word "Hopi" means people of peace, good or moral, and wisely knowing people. All Hopi names are words that have something to do with holiness. You might say that they are people of God. Some people compare the word "Hopi" with the word "saints" as found in the Bible. Tradition has it that the Hopis were once a fierce and warlike people who used to commit many murders and horrible acts. Their tradition of being a people of peace began sometime before the "great star" appeared in the sky. Their conversion to a peaceful way began with a great holy man who taught them that their anger with their brothers was not in harmony with Mother Earth. His teachings were so powerful that the warriors decided never to kill again. They buried their weapons deep in Mother Earth as a symbol to show they would never fight their brothers again. After burying their weapons, the Sun sent other tribes to test them and see if they would return to their old ways. However, the peaceful ones, as they began calling themselves, would not take up their weapons to fight against them. As the others came upon them, they bowed down to Mother Earth, praying that their enemies would have mercy. They were willing to die rather than break their covenant of peace and lose their souls for eternity. Many were killed, but after a while, the enemy became ashamed of killing so peaceful a people and laid down their weapons of war. Some even joined the peaceful Hopi people, burying their weapons to find harmony with Mother Earth again. This is where the old saying "Let's bury the hatchet as a sigh of peace" came from.

The Hopi people were great farmers. They planted crops to feed the starving warriors who were battling around them. When at war, the warring tribes protected the Hopi because of their generosity in growing food for them when they went to war to defend their lands. I remember Bart asking, "Can you see how wise they are, Walker? Did you know that they don't even have curse words in their language? Some people say that the Hopis and the Aztecs are related, and I guess they probably are because they are related to most all of the Indians who lived in this area. The Hopis have claimed that many of the other tribes didn't finish their migration to the peaceful ways."

As I sat with Bart that day, he told me stories of warriors and saints, and my mind carried me to the stories I'd heard and read around the dinner table with Mom and Dad. I asked Bart if he knew of The Book of Mormon. He said that he did. I told him some of the stories I remembered and asked him if he thought there might be a chance that the people in The Book of Mormon could be the same people as the Hopis and the Aztecs. He said he couldn't really say one way or the other, but it appeared that there might be a connection. Bart told me that, on one of his trips to Utah, there was a Book of Mormon in his motel room. He said he started reading it and couldn't put it down until he had finished it. He said he found a number of things in the book that could be related to the traditional stories of the Hopis and many of the other local tribes.

We spent the rest of the morning and part of the afternoon telling stories of the Hopis and comparing them to the Bible and The Book of Mormon. We both agreed that there was much we could learn from the wise men who passed on their history to us. We talked about the fact that life is full of choices, like the choices of the ancient people of that very mesa who put down their weapons and sought harmony and peace. We talked about God and men. Then he taught me something I have carried with me until this very day. He told me of the concern he had for all people. Many people used war to force their beliefs on others. He told me of losing his own father to war and how he had no one with whom to share his father's wisdom. He felt that the only way to keep his father's memory alive was to share his father's advice with me. He asked if I would accept it and pass it on, and I said I would. Bart looked into my eyes and shared his father's words of wisdom.

"Walker, it is important for you to understand that, in this life, there are two ways to go. I've come to the conclusion that the people of peace were like the sons and daughters of Abel, and the people at war were like the sons and daughters of Cain. You can choose the peaceful way and have a happy life no matter what is happening around you. Your peace and joy will be contagious, touching the lives of everybody with whom you come into contact. Or you can choose a warring life of hate, jealously, selfishness, greed, and revenge and become miserable and make everyone around you miserable. You will end up spreading misery wherever you go. I have learned that if you control your anger, everything will get better. However, if you choose not to control your anger, everything will get worse. Walker, look at me, I want you to be a man of peace, and God wants you to be a man of peace also, just as my father wanted me to be a man of peace. I'm telling you this because you are Hopi. You have a heritage of peace." I asked Bart how he knew I was Hopi. Did he know my family? He told me that he didn't know them and that he had no solid evidence leading him to that conclusion, but deep down, something was telling him that it was true. Even if it was not completely accurate, he wanted me to know that I could be like the warring tribes who came upon the peaceful Hopi and put down their swords to join them. Bart continued, "To find harmony in life, it is very important that you always choose the peaceful way. No matter what happens in your life, believe me, you must always choose the peaceful way."

Bart kept his drawing kit in a leather pouch that was decorated ornately with beads and feathers. It was always with him wherever we went. He placed the bag between us. "Let me tell you about Hopis and their close relationship to eagles," he said. "The Hopis will go to the nest of an eagle and take a young chick, which they tether to the roof of their homes so it will never learn to fly. They treat their bird with reverence and hold it in the highest esteem, providing for its every need. In one of their ceremonies, they will sacrifice this bird. They believe that this eagle will ascend into the heavens and take messages to God. They also believe that he has allowed them the honor of using his feathers for their ceremonies. Some of their ceremonial feathers are probably hundreds of years old. They are very sacred and treated with the highest respect."

He handed my feather to me, which he had prepared with beautiful wrappings and decorated with colorful beads. One of the down feathers pulled from the breast of the eagle was attached to the feather. He told me that this down feather represented the voice of God. He said that my eagle will always be part of my life and will carry messages to God. He also said that someday he may guide my soul to heaven.

Walker closed his eyes and held out his arm, as if beckoning the eagle to come and lift him heavenward. He jerked himself out of his trance and continued with the story, as if he had not paused at all.

Bart handed me a leather bag that had a leather string so it could go around my neck and be worn like a necklace. As I took the pouch, the weight of it surprised me. I opened it and found a piece of quartz that had a large streak of gold running through it. The stone was so beautiful! Then he handed me a small cup of water and told me to drop the stone into it. As I took the stone out of the cup, I was amazed at how brilliant the gold became when it was wet. He told me that when I look at the stone, I should always remember how beautiful it is when it's clean. He told me that if I always keep my life clean, I would always be beautiful like the stone. He also told me there was something else in the bag. I turned it over and out came a magnificent pearl. He asked me to always remember that no matter how hard things become in life, I am a pearl of great price.

Bart allowed me to sit quietly for a time to soak up what I had been given. I couldn't help but see the symbolism and the lessons of his gift. He broke the silence with devastating news. "Walker," he said, "I have something difficult to tell you. My job here has come to an end and Bobbie and I will be moving in about six weeks." The words felt like a knife stabbing me in the heart. I immediately broke out crying and couldn't stop. At this point, I felt like sitting up straight and letting myself just slide over the edge of the cliff. I didn't know what I would ever do without Bart and Bobbie! Bobbie was so wonderful! She was someone I could always talk to, someone who could always cheer me up, someone who always had a smile for me, and I realized that I loved her as much as I loved my own mom.

Bart pulled me in close and held me as tight as he could. He didn't say anything, but allowed me to keep on crying. After what seemed like hours, I could feel something wet on my neck and realized Bart was crying too. I wondered how something so wonderful could come to such an abrupt end. I couldn't believe how in one second, just one second, someone's whole life could change from great to completely upside down. I cried so long that my neck, back, and sides hurt, and I just flat ran out of tears. When I couldn't cry anymore, I started sobbing. No matter how hard I tried, I couldn't stop sobbing. Finally I was so worn out I just fell asleep in Bart's arms. I don't know how long I slept in his arms, but when I woke up, it was morning. Bart had, somehow, lifted me off the edge of the cliff, carried me back to camp, and put me into bed.

CHAPTER 8

WORDS OF WISDOM

The next morning, I found Bart sitting at the edge of the cliff watching the morning ground fog, which was covering the valley below and surrendering to the coming sunlight of day. I walked up behind him and threw my arms around his neck. I sat down beside him. I watched him as he fought to compose himself. After a moment, he turned to me and said, "I want to tell you something more about the Hopi. They have a special relationship with the Creator. They believe the Creator allows their elders to see amazing things. For example, did you hear that the Creator showed them Mother Spider spinning her web all over this great nation?" I told Bart I had heard the story but couldn't understand how a spider could spin a web all across this nation. He told me the story. He said the ancient Hopis didn't have any idea either, but when we started planting power poles all across this country and running wires from one pole to another, the elders told all the young men of the tribe that the prophecy was fulfilled. They were told never to depend on Mother Spider's web, for the time would come when it would lose its power and fail. Bart spoke of another prophesy when there would be a time that you could touch a wall and night would turn to day. And a time when water would run uphill and be up on the mesa in abundance, and through the power of the web, the water would flow. Mother Spider's web brought electric power, and the night was turned to day by the flip of a switch on the wall. By this same power, water does flow and run uphill. They were given a strong warning not to depend on Mother Spider's light and the magic of her web, which would make the water flow, because the power of the web would fail. They were told that roads would be built in the sky. As strange as this sounded, the elders never doubted, and they continued to look skyward for the roads. Watching the sky one day, some of the elders looked up and saw a vapor trail from an airplane. The elders simply said, "Now we understand."

Bart paused and looked over the land as the fog gave up its grip on the valley floor below us.

One by one, the trees became more defined in the sunlight. Bart continued as we watched together. He said that he was told by some of the elders that one day there would be rivers all across Indian lands, and he reminded me that we had both been out on the reservation, so we know there is no course for the rivers to follow across this land. He said that he was with a good friend and they were going from Shiprock to Gallup on a very hot day. As they drove, the heat radiated from the pavement and it looked like water flowing. They stopped the car and got out to watch the water vapor rising. Bart asked me if I had ever seen the waves of heat rising off a dirt road, or pavement, and I told him that I had. He told me that the old Hopi prophets had seen the future and that the only way they could explain their visions was to compare what they were seeing to a river.

At this point, Bart went into what appeared to be a daze, and we sat there for quite a while. I told Bart that I had a dream last night and I wanted to tell him about it. In my dream, I saw myself sitting up in my bed looking at the wall of my room, which was covered with a huge American flag. I noticed that there was something slightly different about it. I was then aware that a man was standing by my bed. I thought he looked familiar, but I didn't know his name. I saw that the flag had the same blue square in the top left-hand corner and the seven red stripes separated by six white stripes as our flag does today. The man described its meaning. He told me that the seven red stripes symbolized the seven periods God took to create the earth. They also symbolized a land God had dedicated for those sons and daughters who had stood for valor and bravery. The six white stripes stood for the periods of man that have already passed. The next period, or the seventh period, is when Jesus will come again. When Jesus comes again, He will add the next white stripe onto the flag and usher in the millennium. The white reminds us that the only way to prosper in this land and continue to have God's blessings is to remain innocent and pure. If we don't, God's spirit will not dwell with us and we will lose our freedom.

I was then taken to a place where I saw a group of men, our founding fathers, trying to set up a democracy where the majority would rule. A very tense argument developed because the smaller states wanted to be protected from the tyranny the larger states would impose with majority rule. The battle got so intense that the meeting was about to break apart, dashing the chance of creating a new, united government. The Spirit of God then whispered to Benjamin Franklin, "Let us pray." Benjamin made a wonderful speech about the need for prayer, and George Washington agreed. The meeting was adjourned so all could go to their prayers. When they returned, the atmosphere was changed; God's spirit was able to reside there, and our founders gave us a democratic republic. Then the scene changed, and I was back in my room where an angel was waiting for me. He went to the flag and placed one star, which represented Jesus Christ, in the middle of the blue field. He told me the Savior would raise up another prophet like Moses who would be His mouthpiece and who would be established in this land in the last days. Then he placed twelve stars in a circle around the middle star, which represented the sacred eternal circle. The twelve stars also represented the twelve latter-day apostles who were chosen by the Lord, thus completing the restoration of His church to the earth. He said the blue field signifies our need to be vigilant, to persevere and to maintain justice in order to preserve freedom in this land. God helped prepare our Constitution, which gave us the freedom to worship God as we see fit. The only thing standing between Satan and victory is America and our Constitution. His attack will be merciless.

Bart finally spoke in a real soft voice. He said, "That was a powerful dream. I think you can call it a vision. You know, Walker, I love this country, and I cherish the freedom it gives to all of us."

He then told me that he could see some troubled times coming. He said that even though we have prayer in school every morning right now, there may come a time when prayer isn't allowed in the schools. He said he believed there might even be times when people wouldn't be allowed to talk about God, much less have prayer in school. He was afraid that the time had already come that our elected representatives had stopped representing us and only represented their own special interests and the money that put them into office. He said he believed there's going to be a time when our own Constitution will be dismissed and our Rule of Law ignored. He told me that this kept him up at night and he wanted me to be prepared by staying close to God and by calling upon Him for protection.

I can tell you, I didn't have any idea what he was talking about. He went on to tell me that he thought he could see my future and told me I would be faced with some tough decisions. He warned me to be careful when I make those decisions and to choose the "peaceful way." Then he gave me the eagle feather I had earned and told me to attach all the good things we had done together to it. He said, "When troubled times or tough decisions come into your life, I want you to look at this feather and let it be a reminder that only good and happy things come from making the right choices." He told me from that point on we wouldn't talk about Bobbie and him leaving, and he wanted me to remember only the good things we had done and the wonderful times we'd had together. He said, "Walker, my son, if you do this, you won't feel the hurt. You and I became family the day we met. Parting may feel like we're dying, but you never know when our paths will cross again. Most of the time, when a loved one dies, those who are left behind will only think about what they have lost. It is only when they start remembering the wonderful times they shared that they start to heal. I will need to heal too." Then he put his arm around my shoulder and told me that he didn't want us to grieve anymore. I hugged him again, but I didn't cry this time.

After a moment he asked me for my feather. He took it, and as he caressed it gently, he said, "Just like your ancestors of old, I want you to take this feather and put all of your good memories and all of your decisions on it. Treat it like it will take a message to God but also understand that it is not to take the place of your prayers. The power of the feather is to remind you of all the things you are grateful for, and bring to your memory all the decisions you need to pray about. There will be times when you are going to have to choose between fighting or accepting your situation as inevitable. The image of the feather will help you figure out how to make the best of any situation. There will be times when revenge seems to be yours and may be justified. The presence of the feather is to remind you that revenge belongs to God and nobody else. You know the book you read, The Book of Mormon, is the word of God. I know you also believe that the Bible is the word of God. Keep these books with your feather and always live by what these sacred books teach you."

I was amazed to hear Bart talk of these sacred texts with such reverence, and I asked him if he believed The Book of Mormon was the word of God, why he hadn't been baptized and joined my church. His answer was simple, "Because no one has ever asked me to join." As he stood up and started back toward our camp, I remembered the many times we had gone to church activities and never once invited either Bart or Bobbie to come with us. Then I had a brilliant idea! I got up and chased after him. "If I ask you to join my church, will you join? It would make us more like family." With a warm, gentle, and loving smile he told me he wouldn't join just because I asked him to, but now that I had asked, perhaps he would give it some serious thought. After all, we were brothers connected by our eagle. The hurt vanished.

He told me it was time to get ready to go home and that Bobbie would be waiting for me at the bottom of the mesa. My heart jumped. I asked him when Bobbie had arrived, and he told me that she had been there all along. "She didn't join us because she couldn't bear the thought of being there when I told you that we were going to have to move." Bart said, "Walker, Bobbie and I haven't been able to have children, and you have been like our very own son. In fact, you're the greatest son any man or woman could ever have asked for. Remember, we will always love you."

Bobbie had been there the whole time? Apparently she had spent the whole weekend behind an outcrop of rocks near our camp. I couldn't believe it! I asked if she had seen us catch the eagle, and he said that she certainly had, and that after I had fallen asleep, she scolded Bart for not taking greater precautions. She helped him bind up his wounds and finally got the bleeding stopped. From a distance, she was part of everything we did; plus, she got a lot of reading in.

Well, that was all the motivation I needed, and without thinking about anything else, I started sliding down through the crevasse. Just before I got to the bottom, I remembered my eagle feather. I turned around and scrambled back up the mesa as quickly as I could. I picked up the feather, and as I did so, I noticed that it had some blood on it. As I looked at Bart, I could see that the wound had opened up and his shirtsleeve was soaked with blood. When he gave me my feather, he must have unintentionally sealed his words with his own blood.

When I got to the bottom of the hill, there was Bobbie. I ran to her and hugged her so hard that we both fell down. We had a nice long walk to the car and a wonderful drive home. On the way, we talked about the marvelous things we had done since we met. I'll tell you, nothing could ever get any better than that!

As we drove up to the door, I realized why Mom had been crying when we left. She had been told the dreadful news that they were moving, and I felt sorry for her. She and Bobbie had grown extremely close, and one couldn't get along without the other. What would my poor mom ever do without Bobbie?

Walker said, "Bishop, I have to stop now. I must sleep before taking the rest of my journey. We will start again in the morning."

Walker told me he wasn't looking forward to tomorrow because his memories were about to "turn from heaven to hell." With that, he took a drink of water, rolled over, and went to sleep. I couldn't help but notice how weak Walker was becoming. As he slept, his mouth was moving but no words were coming out. No expressions of pain or discomfort harrowed his brow. Apparently happy memories were running through his mind, and I was looking at a man who had finally found peace. As I went back over to the edge of the mesa to watch the setting sun, I realized that his journey through life may not see another morning. I pondered why God had brought us together and what information was so important that Walker needed others to hear. As the sun set, a voice whispered to my soul, "Like the prophets of old, Walker will not die until his message has been delivered. Bishop, you are the messenger." A profound feeling washed over me. Satisfied, I went back to my bedroll and fell soundly to sleep.

PART TWO

CHAPTER 9

THE NIGHTMARE BEGINS

The next morning I awoke to two surprises. The first was the layer of frost covering the ground, and the second was seeing Walker doing his best to fix me breakfast. I quickly dressed and rushed to his aid only to have him chastise me for not accepting his hospitality. For the past two days, Walker had been so weak he could hardly raise his head off the mat he used as a bed. However, since he considered me to be a guest, he wanted to do everything he could to make me comfortable. His ability to keep going was a constant source of amazement to me.

I stood by the fire and watched him prepare our meal. He took meat and cooked it until it was dry. He then ground it into a coarse powder, mixed it with the native seeds he had collected on the mesa, and used honey as a binder to keep it together. The cold morning air helped it firm up into a thick mass, which he cut into four-by-one-inch squares. This is what he ate twice a day. Even though it looked like a hardened pile of vomit, the flavor was surprising, and I found myself completely satisfied and even savoring the taste of it. A person could do very well on this meal and never feel hungry. As withered and frail as Walker was, he was now moving around, his movements clearly showing his will and his dogged determination. Together, we gathered firewood and collected honey from the rocks just as he had described in his tales about being with Bart on the mesa. Gathering the honey brought to me the realization that this was the area where the story of the eagle feather had originated. The beehive was isolated on the back side of the outcrop of sandstone used for the cistern. There, we found a constant source for honey that was protected from everything but man and moths. To demonstrate his appreciation, Walker made sure the moths did not damage the beehive.

I had always heard that the ancient people had established an easy lifestyle living off the land and camping out all the time. Don't you believe it! Their way of life was demanding, difficult, and dirty, and if their daily foraging for food was unsuccessful, it quickly became miserable.

By now I was fully realizing how demanding, difficult, and dirty it was just to bring needed supplies up onto the mesa. Getting to my pickup required a hard day's walk out of the mountains, not to mention the drive into town. Carrying supplies back to the mesa quickly became enormously burdensome, and each time I returned, I felt like I had been carrying a thousand pounds! I became acutely aware of what I was using because hauling supplies up onto the mesa was exhausting work. I knew Walker had spent the last two winters up there, and I don't think he had ever gone down for supplies. To tell you the truth, I don't know how he survived it, being ill and all, let alone when he was in good health.

Up to that point Walker's and my conversations had been short. Since he didn't look to be in much pain today, I was in hopes of having a little more time with him. Unfortunately, he was not in the mood for talking, so I decided to go fishing.

Since the fishing was good, it was late when I returned. Walker was sleeping, so I fixed the fish for supper. I don't know why, but I stood at the opening of the lean-to he used for a home and watched him for a long time. Deciding not to wake him, I returned to the fire and sat musing at the day's events. As the flames turned into smoldering embers, I decided to retire for the night. Walker was already asleep, and not wanting to disturb him, I decided to kneel under the stars to pray. It was while in the attitude of prayer that a quiet impression came to me: Walker was avoiding me because he didn't know how to go on with his life story. I had the feeling his tale was heading for a turn more painful to him than the physical pain of his illness.

When I woke the next morning, I found Walker sitting in his favorite place on the edge of the mesa. The sun was already high enough to paint the valley below in color. I had learned, from casual conversations with Walker, that the "morning breath of the valley" was one of his favorite rituals, and every morning when his strength would allow, he could be found at the mesa's edge. I went over and sat beside him. Walker looked at me momentarily but didn't speak. Finally, I told him that we didn't have to continue if he wasn't able. His gaze never diverted from the horizon as he whispered, "I have to, but not now. I need to conserve my strength." I got up and went back to my tent, leaving him alone to gather what strength he could to continue his story. It was about noon when Walker called me from my tent and told me he was ready. I returned to the edge of the mesa and sat down beside him.

Our town was real small, and we didn't have missionaries. The church leaders asked Dad and Brother Connor to be special missionaries so they could teach the lessons to Bart and Bobbie. In our church these special missionaries are known as "Seventies." That had to be done before they could be baptized. Even though I wasn't a member of the church, they let me go with them and even let me help teach. It was amazing to hear Bobbie pray; you could feel God's presence it was like He was standing there and she was talking to Him face-to-face. I actually had to open my eyes several times to see if God was in the room. I knew that even if I couldn't see Him, He was there. When Bart and Bobbie decided to get baptized, it seemed like the whole town was excited. I would have given anything to be baptized with them, but the last time Kathy asked permission for me to be baptized, it started a real firestorm with my aunt and uncle, and it was painful for everyone.

Since their permission was necessary for my adoption, we were afraid that bringing up the subject of my baptism would antagonize them even more. So I had to be content with giving a short talk about baptism. Even though I couldn't be baptized, I knew all about it, so giving a talk was a pretty easy task for me. All in all, the baptismal service was wonderful. I am ashamed to say this, but throughout the service I couldn't stop wondering why God had not answered my prayers about being baptized. I had begged and pleaded with Him, and so had Mom, Dad, and Robbie. He refused to answer our prayers, and it really hurt inside to think about it. It was during that service that I decided to stop asking God for anything.

When the time had come for me to give my talk and to bear my testimony, even though God had shown me in several visions what I was supposed to say, I just couldn't do it. I don't remember what I said, but I guess it was okay. I only know that I was glad to get out of there when the service was over. I had come to the conclusion that

God didn't love me or want me even though I had heard a voice, as if someone was in the room, telling me I was loved and to be patient because everything would work out. I believe God spoke to me that day, but I decided to ignore Him, even though I knew what He told me was true. I chose to keep dwelling on the thought that He didn't want me.

Walker shook as he spoke the words, as if the power of God was tearing his soul in two. This was troubling to me. I know if one isn't careful with their thoughts, their mind can lead them to their own personal hell. I was concerned that this was what had happened to Walker. Perhaps this is why he looked so old.

A month later Bart and Bobbie moved." Walker said.

Walker paused. I knew this couldn't be good for him. His countenance was darkening from his conflicted feelings about God and from the emotion he was experiencing from losing Bart and Bobbie.

When he finally spoke again he said, "I'm sorry, but I don't want to talk about this anymore."

I wanted to give explanations and words of comfort but was compelled to keep my mouth shut. The last thing he needed was a sermon or some feeble comparison from my own life. I have seen too many cases where good people let bad thoughts lead them to misery, and I hate to admit it, but I wasn't sure I wanted to go on with his story. I was afraid of what was coming. Without saying a word, I got up and went back to my tent, leaving Walker sitting on the edge of the cliff for the rest of the day. I don't know why, but I didn't come out for supper. I don't believe Walker ate anything either.

I left my tent before daybreak and began tending the fire. We were going to have another cold night, so I quickly inspected Walker's lean-to. He was not in his bed, nor was he on the perch at the edge of the mesa. I was fearful of where I would find him. I quickly moved to the cliff and peered over. "The morning breath of the valley won't happen for a little while yet." The words made me jump, and I turned to see Walker with a load of wood in his arms.

His face was as white as a ghost's. The strain of this physical task racked his body with pain, which was visible everywhere except in his expression.

I moved to help with the work and silently set about assisting him with the chore. As we worked together preparing the campsite and breakfast, Walker turned to me and with a rough voice croaked, "Please don't judge me harshly." I explained to him that it was not my place to judge, that I knew my purpose was to help him pass from this world to the next and, as a witness, to record his words. He smiled and stated simply, "Thanks for giving me some time."

He asked me to help him to the edge of the mesa for his morning ritual. As we sat together, I felt compelled to tell him that I knew he was telling the truth yesterday when he spoke of God's words to him at the baptism. I couldn't help wondering about the great "visions" God had given him. He winced at my comment, and I paused to see if he would continue, or shy away from his story. As I gazed at the features of his ashen face, I began to explain to him that our Savior, Jesus Christ, is fair and just in his judgment of us and that He took upon himself each and every one of our sins. We only have to be willing to give them to him. A single tear rolled down Walker's face as the sun's first golden rays flooded the valley below. He smiled and said, "I think I'm ready to continue."

Baseball season was starting. I had had two great years, and I was ready for this one. My pitching was greatly improved, and I had mastered the curve ball to the inside. In the first game of the season, I walked three and gave up one hit, which gave them only one run. My team carried me off the field on their shoulders, and my head was so big I'm surprised they could even lift me.

Monday at practice, I was introduced to a new boy who had moved up from California. He had been a pitcher for the last three years, and he was going to back me up. As I watched him warm up, I realized that he was really good, and I mean REALLY GOOD!

All week I spent every minute I could practicing. I threw balls into a bucket, which was the diameter I wanted for my strike zone. I threw so hard that I knocked the bottom out of it. By the end of the week I was ready!

As I stood on the pitcher's mound, I made up my mind I wasn't going to try anything fancy, just straight down the line as hard as I could. No one was going to be carried off that field but me. I put everything I had into my first pitch, and felt something explode within me. I saw a bright flash and then everything went black. I was told the batter hit a line drive, which came right back to me like a bullet, shattering my collarbone and one rib and cracking two more. The next thing I knew, I was in an ambulance heading for Grand Junction. The pain was worse than anything I had ever imagined, and it got worse with every breath I took. I was given a sedative, which knocked me out, but then I dreamed about the pain. All I wanted was my mother, not realizing that she was on the field moments after I went down and had been by my side the whole time. The wish I had made before the game had come true; I was the only one carried off the field that night. And I found out what real torture is: an upper body cast and an itch you can't reach!

When I finally got back to school, the coach asked me to be the bat boy so I could still be part of the team. It was almost as much torture as the itch under the cast. I sat there, game after game, and watched some of the best pitching in the world. With every game, the new boy got better, stronger, and closer to pitching a perfect game. I got to where I hated that guy! Funny thing is, I can't even remember his name now.

When I got my cast off, I was told I would be a backup pitcher and that I would take his position in right field. I had played this position before, and I was really fast, so nothing ever got past me. Big deal! No one could hit off him! I could have taken Mom's rocking chair and at least been comfortable while I was out there in right field. We only lost the second game of the season 0 to 1. They got lucky on the first pitch of the game with a home run, but we won the championship game by four runs. It was the best season our league ever had!

Next year the nightmare continued. I practiced for weeks before the season started, only to fill the backup role for him. I couldn't touch him. He overpowered everyone he faced. My attitude grew worse as the season progressed, and by the third or fourth game it reached its peak. He was on fire! No walks, no hits, and two outs with the last batter having two strikes. It was the bottom of the ninth, and somehow the batter connected with the ball and sent a high pop-up to me. I didn't have to move, just hold my glove out and let the ball drop in. I don't know why, but I let the ball just slide out of my glove and fall to the ground. I stared at it a moment before picking it up. The batter, running like a cheetah, rounded second, and was almost to third when

I finally threw the ball in. I could have lobbed it to home and might have put the runner out, but I threw to the pitcher instead. It was very close, but the umpire called the batter safe.

The next batter struck out on three straight pitches and we won the game! The celebration had begun at home plate, but the pitcher remained standing on the mound looking at me. His look caught me off guard. He wasn't angry like I would have been. He looked hurt, like he had lost a friend. That was bad enough, but what was worse, Mom was standing on first base with her hands on her hips. I hadn't fooled her for a second. I didn't go with the rest of the team, but went straight to her. Her only words were, "Walker, what have you done?" She didn't have to say anything more. I knew from her expression my baseball days were over.

Mom continued going to the games but never asked me to go with her. After a few weeks, Curley, our coach, and the pitcher came over to the house and told me they would like me to still be part of the team. The pitcher told me he had no hard feelings and he would like to have me there to pull him out of the ditch when he needed help. Curley told him he knew Kathy well enough to know that I would not be playing for the rest of the year. He asked me if I would continue as the bat boy. That way I could still be part of the team. If they hadn't been so kind and sincere, I would have taken this offer as a slap in the face. I asked Curley about my being an assistant to the assistant coach. "After what you did, how are you going to talk Kathy into rewarding you by letting you become even an assistant to the assistant coach?" Curley asked. Then he said, "Well, kid, if you can do it, you got it." Reluctantly, I followed the rule of never asking Mom and Dad for anything I knew they would have to say no to. I really had only one option, so I humbled myself and took the bat boy position. It turned out I had a great time being part of an undefeated team. My attitude changed, and I developed a massive hunger to be a team player and not the glory hog of the team.

My dog, Scotty, was getting old and was having a hard time keeping up with me while I was delivering papers. It was getting to the point where he was beginning to slow me down. I tried to make him stay home, but somehow, he always got out. One day, I was in a real hurry and I yelled at him and tried to make him go home. He would only back off long enough for me to get started and then I would look back and he was following me again. After about the fifth time, I got mad. I jumped off my bike, picked up a rock, and threw it at him, hitting him just behind his shoulder. He yelped and ran behind a car and I took off as fast as I could to get away from him. Then it hit me, what on earth was I doing? He was the best and most loyal friend I had ever had. What had I done? I slammed on my brakes, spun around, and headed back to find him. I called to him, but he wouldn't come. I could see him peeking from behind the car, and as I tried to get closer to him, he went to the next car. I reached the point where I couldn't stand it anymore, so I just sat down and started to cry. I hated myself! After a few minutes, I felt a wet nose and a scratchy tongue on my face. I grabbed him around the neck, pulled him into my lap, and just sat there crying.

From that time on, when Scotty started slowing down, I parked the bike and we walked the rest of the route together. We stopped now and then so I could take some time to just pet my wonderful and forgiving companion.

As tears ran down my cheeks, he told me "Bishop, I have come to realize that it was then I learned unconditional forgiveness and love. I'm only now realizing the impact Scotty made on me."

As Walker spoke, the tears were flowing uncontrollably, and I found myself getting emotional with him. I was finding that he was becoming a part of me; I was starting to see what he was seeing and feel what he was feeling. The stories were as exhausting for me as I'm sure they were for him. Walker continued.

Not more than three weeks after I hit Scotty with the rock, we were on our way home after finishing my route. We had about three blocks to go and a big black dog came dashing out from between a couple of cars. He grabbed on to my leg, which caused my bike to flip over, throwing me onto the pavement and peeling some of the skin off my left hand and knee. At that instant, Scotty, who was only half the other dog's size, latched on to him and wouldn't let go. He had the dog by the neck just under the ear. The black dog shook him violently but couldn't shake him loose. And by the time I reached them, Scotty had almost choked the dog to the ground. As I pulled Scotty off him, the dog swung around and grabbed me by the arm tearing my arm open a little above the wrist. Then Scotty attacked him again. Before I knew what was happening, I found myself on the ground in the middle of the two fighting dogs. As I looked up, I remember seeing Scotty's shoulder being ripped wide open and blood spurting everywhere! It splattered into my eyes and burned like fire! Suddenly, I felt someone grab me by the leg and pull me out from under the dogs. The lady who grabbed me had a bucket of hot water, which she poured on the dogs to stop the fight. I'm sure glad she knew what to do! Scotty not only had his shoulder torn open but also his eye, part of his ear, and cheek. . The lady, who owned the black dog, started beating him viciously with the bucket until he finally put his tail between his legs and ran over to his kennel. The lady put the dog back into his kennel and checked the doors on the other dog's kennels. After securing the dogs, she returned to us, scooped Scotty up in her arms, and put him in the backseat of her car. She then wrapped her sweater around my arm as she helped me into the front seat and drove us to the doctor's office. Since we didn't have a vet in Uravan, the town's medical doctor often took on that job. He started looking at my wounds first, but I insisted that he help Scotty. Although I was a bloody mess, I didn't feel any pain. He told me that Mrs. Gore, the black dog's owner, would take care of Scotty while he worked on me, and he assured me that she was as good as most vets.

I was already stitched up by the time Mom and Dad arrived at the office, so Dad started helping the doctor and Mrs. Gore with Scotty. Scotty was really torn up. I was so worried about him that I didn't notice that my wrist was throbbing like crazy. I started to cry, and Mom took me in her arms and held me. The doctor had given me something for pain, and as hard as I tried, I couldn't stay awake. When I finally woke up, I was home and Scotty was in a box beside the bed. Dad later cut out the side of the box and put Scotty on the bed with me. He had lost an eye, and we had to carry him outside to go to the bathroom.

When I went on my route, Scotty tried to follow me even though he could hardly walk. Dad told me to keep the door closed so he wouldn't get out of the room and ultimately find a way out of the house. I was very bad about leaving doors open, which worried me as well as the rest of the family, and it wasn't too long before I forgot and not only left the bedroom door open but also the kitchen door as well. As I was going down the road I looked behind me out of habit, and to my surprise, there was Scotty trying to catch up with me. He was a ways behind me, and as I watched him, I could also see Mrs. Ashe driving down the hill leading from the highway toward the A and B Block housing areas. She lived in B Block. At the bottom of the hill was a sharp curve to the right going into B Block, and I knew she would be turning onto her street right where Scotty was, turning into his blind side. I started yelling, screaming, and jumping up and down to get her attention. She saw me, but unfortunately she didn't see Scotty. She turned her car into B block and ran right over him! I ran to them and found Mrs. Ashe's three little girls screaming and crying, and Mrs. Ashe was trying to deal with them and help Scotty all at the same time. We took Scotty home, and Mom took him to the doctor immediately. There was nothing he could do. He told us Scotty had internal injuries and it was only a matter of time. I knew someone who could do something for him, and that was God. Although I wasn't sure He was willing to help me, perhaps He would be willing to help Scotty. I had gone with Dad when he had given some blessings to very sick people, and I had seen, firsthand, what God can do. Dad told me that blessings and miracles are sacred and I shouldn't talk about them. But again, I can tell you from firsthand knowledge that I know what God can do and I knew that Scotty would be no challenge for Him. I went out into the waiting room, got down on my knees, and asked God to heal Scotty. I promised Him that if He would, I would never be bad again. I didn't feel good about the prayer, but I knew He could heal Scotty if He wanted to. The doctor sent us home with Scotty, and he died in my arms on the way. I was devastated! When we got home, I went straight to my room, got down on my knees, and yelled at God, "I hate you and I will never pray to you again!" I meant it! God had allowed my very best friend to die! The next day, we buried Scotty up on the rim of the canyon.

I found out later that the big black dog was part of a pack used for hunting cougars and he was just doing what he was trained to do. The next week when I went by the house with the kennels, all the dogs, and

even the cages, were gone. I never delivered another paper and never
. . .

Walker stopped short. At that point, he got up and walked over to the fire. He didn't say another word the rest of the evening. It was for the best, because I don't believe I would have been able to continue. I soon retired to my tent and slept fitfully. I dreamed of the boy, Walker, losing his dog and taking it out on God. It was a nightmare I won't soon forget.

CHAPTER 10

SNATCHED

After hours of fitful sleep and crazy dreams, I decided to sit up and write the impressions I had received thus far before continuing on with Walker. He had become such an important part of me that I knew we had been very good friends in spirit before we came to this earth. Now we were together, once again, and I was playing an integral role in his life here on earth. The most troubling aspect of Walker's story, to that point, was his rejection of God. Every time I have encountered someone who blames God for his circumstances, I have found a life torn to pieces.

I desperately wanted to stop my young friend from condemning God in any way. I don't know why God sometimes lets things happen the way He does, but I do know that at certain times you can sense God's closeness to you and it seems like you can reach out and touch Him. His still, small voice comes through so loudly and clearly that you know He is right there with you, talking to you. Other times, it feels like God leaves you standing with your arms outstretched and He seems no closer to you than the distant stars. However, I believe the day will come when all the answers to our questions will be made clear. That will be the day when we pass from this life into the next and then have the opportunity to learn from the Master. What makes me believe? The moments when I have been in need and His still, small voice has penetrated my soul and brought me assurance of the truth.

The silence of the night slowly made its retreat, and as the predawn light chased the shadows, I left my tent to stoke the fire. As I did this, I heard an ominous moan coming from Walker's lean-to. Startled, I rushed to the lean-to and discovered that Walker was racked with fever, his face ashen *and ghostly. The sight of him was shocking! Walker had vomited several times during the night, and were it not for the faint moans, I would have believed him to be dead. I didn't know of any way I could help him, and I wondered what in the world I was to do! We were days away from any kind of medical care, and it would have been a tremendous task to get help onto the mesa. I knew there was only one thing I could do. As a man ordained unto the Priesthood of God, I knelt beside him and placed my hands on his head. I asked God that if it was time for Walker to go, to please take him quickly so his suffering would end. However, if it wasn't his time to go, I prayed that he would regain his strength so we could complete our mission together. I closed the blessing in the name of Jesus Christ, satisfied that I had done all I could do. I tried to make Walker more comfortable and to get him to eat something, but he was still unable to keep anything down. He was as cold as ice and sweating at the same time. I was afraid that Walker would die, and I didn't know what I was going to do with his body! I remembered that Brigham Tea was an herb that grew wild in the area and that the settlers had used it for all kinds of medicinal purposes. I proceeded to make some of the tea and got as much of it into him as I could. I crouched by Walker's bed all that day and through the night hoping for the best but preparing for the worst. By morning I was seeing definite signs of recovery.*

My spirits lifted as I continued to nurse him. He finally woke at the end of the second day and thanked me profusely for my efforts. I was very relieved, but I was also dead on my feet.

The next morning I arose to find Walker sitting at the edge of the cliff waiting for the sun to rise. His cheeks were hollow and his face was still ashen, but other than that, it was like the last three days had never happened. He just sat there smiling at me and asked if I was ready to continue with the story. I replied, "Only if you don't fall over dead while I'm taking notes." He attempted to smile and began again.

Mom and Dad started looking for my birth mother soon after I was placed with them. They needed to find her to see if she would sign the papers for my adoption. I don't know how much money they spent hiring people to look for her, but I know it was a lot! One afternoon my dad's partner, Dale Connor, had a meeting with Dad about selling one of their mines. I did my best to listen without being detected. Mr.

Connor wanted to set up an account in Mexico with his part of the money, and he said it would be in both their names. That way Dad could have access to it if he ever needed it. I thought that sounded strange, but what did I know? I remember Dad telling Dale it was his money and he should use it for his family, but Dale told Dad he could count on the money. When Dale Connor set his mind to something, there was no changing it.

Shortly after their meeting, I was told we had another hearing in Arizona concerning the proposed adoption, and I had that sick feeling in my stomach. After almost nine years of court hearings, I knew better than to talk about our chances. It was the only trip Mom, Dad, and I ever made together when no one talked. Consequently, it was a long, hard, and depressing journey. When we entered the courtroom, my aunt and uncle were there with their slimy lawyer and another man I had never seen. The man introduced himself as the attorney for the tribe. Mom and Dad had our attorney, and apparently someone from the tribe also. My aunt and uncle's lawyers didn't spend much time making their case, and before I knew it, we had our turn. Our new attorney from the tribe wanted to put me on the stand, but since the judge wouldn't allow it, our attorney started calling character witnesses. I was amazed to see that most of the town of Uravan had made the trip to help us out. After hours of testimony supporting my family, our attorneys again asked that I be allowed to speak on my own behalf. The other side objected, and again, I was not allowed to speak. Upset, I stood and asked the judge just who's life did he think he was dealing with anyway? I was immediately removed from the courtroom, and the hearing continued without me for the rest of the day.

The following day our lawyers asked me to remain outside the courtroom because my outburst the day before had not helped our case. I wanted to be in the courtroom in the worst way, but I reluctantly did what I was told. About noon, I was summoned into the courtroom to hear the judge's ruling. The judge did his best to explain his ruling to me, but I didn't focus on him much after I heard the words "in favor of the plaintiff." Much of what was said had to do with some of the papers Mom and Dad had signed when they first picked me up from the reservation. Apparently, they had never had the legal right to keep me. Even though I didn't understand everything, this much

I did understand. I was to be given into the custody of my aunt and uncle. I couldn't think or even breathe! When Mom heard the ruling, she jumped up and ran out of the courtroom, and Dad slumped in his seat. Robbie went after Mom, who needed him more than she had ever needed anyone in her life. I sat down in her chair next to Dad while the judge finished giving his instructions. I didn't hear anything they were saying. Thoughts raced through my mind. What could I do? I could run away, or perhaps I could figure out a way to make them pay for taking me from my family. I remembered clearly how I used to put foster parents through pure hell when I was little. I could easily do that again.

When we left the courtroom, we found our car surrounded by shocked and crying people. They all wanted to hug me and tell me how sorry they were, but I didn't want to have anything to do with anyone. I just wanted to get out of there! When we got to the highway, Dad stopped the car. He and Mom started talking about the possibility of going south to Mexico. Mom said there were some things she needed from the house, so we headed north. Robbie and I looked at each other with big smiles on our faces when we realized their plan was to make a run for it. We could both learn Spanish and do whatever else we needed to do. In fact, Mom and Dad could already speak Spanish. They started talking like magpies as they went over the different scenarios, and Robbie and I soon fell asleep. This was more like our family!

When we got back to Uravan, Dad drove straight to the post office because Mom was expecting a very important letter. The letter was there, but for some reason she was afraid to open it. After hesitating for a few minutes, she finally opened it. Robbie had tested positive for multiple sclerosis, and the doctor recommended that he start medical treatment as soon as possible. I watched as all the color drained out of their faces; the letter slipped from her hands and floated to the floor of the car. Mexico was no longer an option. As we pulled into the driveway, I saw Fat Man and two women I didn't recognize waiting for us to arrive home so they could pick me up. Dad was angry when they met him at the door, and he refused to let them in. The Fat Man explained that the court had issued papers and he had no choice. There was a hint of kindness in his voice as he suggested that if we needed more time he could go and have the sheriff deliver the papers. This would give us two or three more hours together before I had to leave. Dad and Mom could tell that Fat Man really didn't want to do what he had to do, so Dad calmed himself and let them in. Before Fat Man and one of the ladies could get through the door, the other lady pushed them out of the way and burst into the room. She was even fatter than Fat Man and she sneered as she spoke. She pointed to the bedrooms and ordered me to get my things, now, because she had no intention of spending the night! Uravan did not have a motel, and with the oil rigs and the mines, there were no rooms in Naturita, Nucla, or Norwood. It was already 8:00 p.m. Oh, I thought, where was Scotty when I needed him? I told her to shut her fat mouth! I would get my things when I was darn good and ready and it wouldn't be tonight! I wasn't going to take anything from her because, right then, I had nothing to lose. I went over to the couch and folded my arms and everyone could see I wasn't going to move.

Dad explained that the journey from Arizona was long and we were exhausted. He asked them if they could give us until tomorrow, around noon, to organize my stuff. Fat Man and the nicer of the two ladies quickly agreed and started for the door, but the evil one insisted that I come with them tonight. Dad asked them to please come and sit at the table and talk about it.

Fat Man and the nice lady agreed, but not the evil one. She kept demanding, and I kept sitting. She went to the table and started pounding on it, screaming profanities that we never used in our home, or anywhere. At first Dad asked her, politely, to sit and calm down. Then he got quiet. I looked up to see the color leave his face as the evil one continued her tirade. I got up from the couch and went over and stood by him. I knew they were in danger because I could feel the heat coming from his body. He was staring at the table so his eyes would not give his intentions away, and I could tell he was prepared to make his move. Fat Man tried to calm the evil one down, but she wouldn't stop. The nice lady appeared to be embarrassed, and she left the house and went to the car. I looked at Mom, and her expression told me exactly what she was thinking. Inside her head she was screaming at God, telling him he had better let her know that I would be all right or she would turn Buddy loose on Fat Man and the evil one. I knew that when Dad got through with them, we would have to make a run for

Mexico for sure! Just then, Robbie came out of the bedroom. I could see the fear in his eyes as he looked first at Dad, and then at me, as if begging for my help. Out of the corner of my eye, I could see Buddy's hand sliding toward his boot, which was where he carried his knife. That was the second time I had a vision of what was about to happen, and it wasn't pretty. With the picture of Robbie's eyes begging for help, and Mom screaming at God swimming in my mind, I heard a voice in my mind clearly say, "Do it, and do it now." I turned to Dad and gently placed my hands on his bald head and kissed it. I bent down close to his ear and said in a soft voice, "You can't do this, Dad. You have to take care of Mom and Robbie. I will be all right. You and Mom will always be my mom and dad no matter what." I could feel his spirit and his heart break under my hands. For the first time, my mom was screaming at the God she loved so much, and Robbie was petrified with fear. It appeared that I was destroying everything I loved just by living! I could see full well that it was time for me to take the decision out of their hands. Fat Man got up, left the room, and went to the car. Meanwhile, the evil one told me to get my stuff and to hurry up about it. I told her to drop dead, that I didn't have anything there because everything belonged to Robbie. I told her that if we didn't leave right now, I wouldn't be going with her. She got her massive body up out of the chair and waddled toward the door. As I reached the door, I turned and looked at Dad. Mom had her head on his shoulder, and I could see that his face was empty and expressionless; he was just the empty shell of a once powerful and great man. I turned and left the house without even saying goodbye. When I got to the car, I opened the door for the evil one because that is what Mom would have expected me to do. I realized that this was the second time I had left a home without taking my coat, and once again, I didn't go back for it. As we pulled away, I turned to see Robbie crying in the doorway. When we were on the road, the evil one smugly commented, "I told you we could pick him up and get on our way before morning."

At that point, I realized the only way to get these people out of my life was to kill them. As I sat there listening to her flapping her stupid yap, my mind drifted to my Uncle Glenn who, you might say, took Bart's place in my life after Bart moved away. Glenn joined the military at the beginning of WWII and was sent to France to help build up the French resistance. For over two years he went out every week and killed anywhere from two to six Nazis. At least once a week he was able to destroy something important to the Nazi war effort, like communications, ammunition dumps, etc. Glenn would pick a spot where he could kill one Nazi and then leave his body lying in plain sight. When other soldiers came to see what happened, he would kill them too. He told me that, one time, he killed ten in the same spot. Glenn said that the Nazis went crazy because they thought the whole town was involved. Their solution was to execute twice as many citizens as he had killed and to leave them lying in the street as a deterrent to the further killing of Nazi soldiers. Glenn said he didn't feel too bad about this because he felt the people were better off dead than living under Nazi terror, and it was great for recruiting resistance fighters. The reason they hadn't found Glenn was because he had been hiding in one of the officer's attics for two years. While the Nazis were searching the whole town for him, he was safe and sound. He said it got to the point where the Nazis were shooting some of their own officers in order to intimidate the other officers into stopping the resistance once and for all. Glenn felt like he was God's instrument in getting rid of the Nazi SOBs because he considered them to be "children of Satan." This was a different point of view from my dad's, who didn't talk about the war because he felt like he had killed Heavenly Father's children when he had fought in the Philippines. Uncle Glenn taught me to hide in plain sight, and we played games where we would see how close we could get to people without being seen. It was easy at night, but we also did it in full daylight. He told me that when he and Dad were little boys, they would stay at their grandparents' house during summer vacation. Their grandparents owned a trading post on the Apache reservation, which was where they met Crazy Charlie, the old Apache who worked at the trading post. Crazy Charlie's father had been a great warrior who had refused to surrender and move on to the reservation. He had taken Charlie on the warpath with him torturing and killing every white settler he could find. He also killed every Apache he came across who had surrendered because he felt they were not only weak but also traitors to the Apache way of life. Because of this killing spree, the army put all of their resources into hunting the two renegade Apaches. Charlie's father appeared to have the diyi power of being invisible.

Many times the pony soldiers, who were the cavalry hunting renegade Apaches, would pass by him in their search and would never see him. When Crazy Charlie was in his tenth year, his father's diyi power failed. Twelve pony soldiers on patrol suddenly appeared, and when they got close, Charlie's father hid him in some trees. He then proceeded to lead the soldiers away. When it seemed to Charlie's father that he had lost the soldiers, he went to a nearby ranch to steal a couple more horses, and that's where he was captured and killed. A few of the soldiers who were still looking for Charlie returned and made camp right underneath him. He sat in the tree and was totally concealed while watching them finish their evening meal. Ten of the soldiers retired for the night, and when they were asleep, Charlie killed all ten of them. Because of his diya power of being invisible he was able to walk right past the two night guards without them ever knowing that he had been there. Because of this, he thought that, like his father, he had the power to be invisible. However, within a few days the army found Charlie and chased him to the edge of a cliff. Rather than surrender, he decided to jump. The soldiers assumed he was dead and decided to leave him there to rot. Meanwhile, Buddy's grandfather, Jake, who was working with the soldiers as a scout, couldn't stand the thought of leaving Charlie's body at the bottom of the cliff. When he went back to get Charlie he found that Charlie was still alive but badly broken up. Jake decided to take him back to his trading post where he nursed him back to health. Charlie told Grandpa that while he was unconscious at the bottom of the hill, Yusan, the god of the beginning and the creator of all things, came to him. He thought that Yusan would surely take him to Deg-oz-none, "The Pretty Place" but instead, he was taken to the place the whites call "Hell." He said there was no fire there, just darkness and many souls who were moaning loudly and giving off bloodcurdling screams for no apparent reason. Each person appeared to be at war trying to gain power and control over all the others. Charlie said the smell in that place was worse than the smell of decaying flesh. Yusan told him he did not get involved in conflicts there. Charlie took Yusan by the hand and told him he did not want to stay there. Yusan said only good people that love Me and obey my commandment to love God, love your neighbor and do no harm to anyone can go to the Pretty Place. Yusan said Charlie could go to the Pretty Place but

Charlie would live in pain all the rest of his days on earth. The only exception would be the day of his death when Yusan came to take him home. He told Charlie he was never to know a woman. Yusan stated that the seed of Charlie's ancestors would stop with him. He was also never to use his Apache name or to say his father's name again. Charlie knew that he had done many vile things, so he told Yusan he would do what he had been told to do. Because Charlie was so crippled up, the army decided he was no longer a threat to anyone. They figured he had gotten just what he deserved. Despite his handicaps, Charlie was able to make a living by working at the trading post and teaching the army how to break mustang ponies. He became known as "Crazy Charlie" because of his crippled appearance and the wild stories he told. Bishop all this is true but you will not find any record of it. Charles's father drove the army crazy. They put every soldier they had in the field 24/7 but he killed and tortured at will. Charlie and his father would run their horses until they died. Charlie and his father would cut them open and take what they needed for substance and either catch or steal more horses and keep going. There was no way the army could keep up with them. The army had a hard time getting any soldiers to stand guard duty because he would kill them. The ranchers and farmers were leaving by the groves. It is my understanding the reason the military wiped out all the records is because if there were 500 lone wolves like Charles's father the Apache would still own all their territory. They in no way they wanted him to become a martyr. During the summers, Buddy and Glenn spent a lot of time at the trading post where Crazy Charlie taught them to track game, break horses, and how to become invisible. That knowledge saved their lives many times during World War II.

Glenn told me Crazy Charlie said that sometimes an Apache's power would leave him and he would have to go on raids to get it back. He would kill and torture until his power came back, and then he would return home and life would be good. When I was taken from my house, I felt that my power had left me just like the Apaches Uncle Glenn had told me about. All I knew was that the evil one who had taken me was as much of a devil as any Nazi.

I always carried a six-inch fish knife with me, which I had converted into a switch blade because real switch blades were against the law. I put the cover from a book of matches in the blade guide so the blade wouldn't close all the way. When I pulled it out of my back pocket, the point of the blade would catch on my pants pocket and be fully opened by the time it cleared my pocket. It was better than a switch blade, and it was legal.

The evil one just wouldn't shut up, and all I knew was that I didn't want to hear that screeching voice anymore! As I reached for my knife, I could hear Bart's voice telling me to take the Hopi path of the peaceful way. Shocked, I sat back in the seat. The evil one kept on and I went for my knife again. I had my hand on my knife when Mom's face flashed before my eyes. I didn't care! All I wanted to do was to cut that woman's stupid throat and shut her up! I had my knife blade open when Mom's face flashed in front of me again, but this time it was different. She had a way of flashing you a warning with her eyes that told you she meant business. This was like a slap in the face, and I sat back in the seat with the knife by my side. Dad and Glenn had taught me how to kill efficiently, if I ever had to, and Mom and Bart had taught me how to control the extremely powerful impulse to kill out of anger.

Then the evil one made a comment about Buddy and Kathy trying to steal Indian children. I had taken all I was going to take from her! I sat forward and asked, "Do you know why I agreed to go with you?" She started to say something vile and I stopped her. "Do you know what Dad did in the war? He was a commando and he killed hundreds in combat with only his hands and a knife. Didn't you see his hand going to his boot?"

"Your words don't scare us," she said with a tightlipped grin on her face.

I leaned over the front seat and with a voice not my own but that of a cold-blooded Nazi mass murderer, which chilled me clear to the bone, I said to Fat Man, "You were seconds away from having your head bashed in by his hands." Then to the evil one I said, "And you from having your throat slit open with his knife." As I said that, I used my left hand to grab Fat Man's neck. At the same time I ran my right hand across the evil one's throat.

Suddenly, Walker sat straight up on his mat and screamed, "Shut up! I can't take it anymore!" and it was like his muscles exploded! His body straightened, becoming as stiff as a board. His knees jerked convulsively as he drew them up to his chest. I could see the muscles in his arms and legs congeal into big knots the size of grapefruits and then release with a violent motion. I realized that he was having a convulsion, and I stood there totally stunned and unable to move. At that instant, I could hear his teeth pop like a .22 bullet going off, and I realized that I needed to get something into his mouth before he bit off his tongue. All I could find was a small stick, but it appeared that there was no way on earth I would be able to get it into his mouth. Since Walker was thrashing around violently, there was no way I could hold him still. Finally, I threw myself across his chest and tried to open up his mouth; his teeth were still popping and grinding. With both of my hands, I pried open his mouth and inserted the little stick, but the pressure of his jaws broke the stick in half! I was afraid that he would choke, so I rolled him over hoping he wouldn't swallow the piece of stick in his mouth. This appeared to be a big mistake because he started to smash his face into the sandstone underneath himself, which scratched his face and caused his nose to bleed. I was in a total panic! I tried to give him a priesthood blessing but couldn't even remember the words! In frustration I stood up, raised both hands toward the heavens, and yelled, "Father, you have to stop this now!" Thankfully, my pleas were heard because Walker started to calm down immediately. I was trembling so badly I could hardly walk! When his jaws started to relax, I was able to remove the stick from his mouth. Walker's eyes were as glazed over and his body as lifeless as any corpse I had ever seen, and I have seen a few in my time. Slowly he came back to his senses and told me he was able to understand everything I had said. I was greatly relieved knowing that Walker was going to be okay, at least for the time being. His face was scratched up, and he had sand, blood, and dirt all over himself. When I offered to get some water to clean him up, he said in a firm voice I didn't recognize, "Sit down and start writing! I have to finish this!" Dutifully, I sat down, and as I opened up my notebook, I noticed blood running down the page. It was then I realized that Walker had bitten off the tip of my little finger!

He continued from the exact spot we had left off before he went into convulsions, as if nothing had ever happened.

She screamed, and Fat Man almost wrecked the car. I sat back in my seat and whispered that they had better not fall asleep because I might finish the job. I thought, "Why should Dad do the killing when

I can do it myself?" No one spoke during the remainder of the trip. When I occasionally locked eyes with Fat Man in the rearview mirror, he quickly looked away, not wanting to interact with me in any way.

Meanwhile, the nice lady sat quietly with me in the backseat. I told her she had nothing to fear because she was not like the two up front. She smiled nervously as she put her hands in her lap, never once looking at me. I realized that here I was at the age of fifteen and I had more power than I had ever known. It felt GREAT! With this thought in mind, I laid my head back and fell asleep. I had successfully begun my reign of terror!

CHAPTER 11

REVENGE

As I slept, I dreamed of the Apaches and the stories my dad and Uncle Glenn had told me about them. I saw myself as an Apache warrior going on a raid to get my power back, and I heard the bloodcurdling screams of my victims. I pictured myself as Uncle Glenn killing the Nazi soldiers by the dozens, and I felt the power and satisfaction of having completed my missions successfully. It was a good feeling and I reveled in it.

When I woke up, I thought back to the years I had lived in fear of being taken away from my family, and the torment the tribal representatives had put us through all those years. Now they had taken everything I had ever cared about away from me. When I had left the house, I felt totally powerless, but my actions in the car had made me feel powerful, reinforcing everything my dad and Uncle Glenn had told me about the Apache warriors. Now that I had gotten a little taste of power, I knew that I wanted more.

We drove all night and into the next afternoon and when Fat Man finally stopped the car, it was to let the lady in the backseat off at her home. I pretended I was still asleep, but when the lady opened the door to get out of the car, I grabbed her arm and gave her a wicked smile. She appeared startled and fearful as she quickly pulled away from me and ran all the way to her front door.

Then Fat Man and the evil one took me to my uncle's place. When they pulled up to the house, I got out on the evil one's side. I opened her door and she just sat there, white with fear, as I reached across her lap and took her purse. I took her wallet out and pulled out her driver's license. Then, in a menacing voice, I said, "Every night before you go to sleep, think about what you've done to me and my family. I know where you live now, so you'd better keep on the lookout for me because I may change my mind about letting you live!" I waived her license in front of her face and continued, "I can assure you that, one day, you will get what's coming to you!" As I watched her almost pass out, I threw her purse at her, slammed the door, and walked backward toward the house, drawing my fingers across my throat as I walked. I reveled in my newfound power! I could have done anything I wanted to do to them and they wouldn't have been able to stop me. I had more power than I had ever known, and it was totally intoxicating!

As Walker related the story to me, I could see a bloodlust in his eyes. This wasn't the same Walker who had been sitting before me begging me with kindness and compassion to continue. The person he was describing was a cold and heartless creature. In my mind I pictured those gentle eyes of his as he had asked me not to judge him harshly, telling me that he knew of Jesus's kindness and mercy from firsthand experience. Looking at him become the beast he described in his story was frightening, and I felt the impulse to run. Walker was still talking, but I didn't hear what he was saying because I had closed my eyes and was telling God my concerns. As I questioned my need to remain, I heard a distinct voice echoing in my head, "Leave if you must, but you are here on My errand." I felt an instant calm sweep over me and I was able to return my attention to Walker and his story.

He hadn't noticed my struggle as he continued to tell me about his aunt and uncle and their two boys greeting him at his arrival.

They were nervous and unsure of themselves, and I'm certain they could sense the power I now had. My uncle's name is Jimmie Begay and my aunt's name is Annie. The oldest boy was Tommy, age thirteen, and the younger one was Jack, age eleven. They told me I would have two brothers now, but I told them I only had one brother and they had taken me away from him when he needed me the most. I told them I was hungry and tired and only wanted them to give me something to eat and to show me where to sleep. Like obedient servants, they did as I asked.

After I had eaten, I went to the bedroom and lay down. I was surprised to find their kindness so comfortable and inviting, and this gave me the feeling that I was somehow betraying my family in Colorado. I was almost asleep when my aunt knocked on the door and asked to come in. She sat on the bed. "Walker," she said, "I hope you understand that we never wanted to take you away from the Smiths. It was your mother who asked us to help her find you, and the tribe that did not want the Smiths to keep you. The last time I saw your mother she made me promise I would find you and bring you home, and that promise has haunted me all these years. Jimmie is on the Tribal Council and we were asked to take you in." I remained motionless on the bed, not watching her and doing my best to be invisible. She took my hand in hers. "Please give us a chance." Her voice was so sincere it made me squirm a little.

"Will you take me to see my family?" I asked. My words sounded like they had come from someone else.

"We can't afford to go often, but we will try to take you to see your family as often as possible." She smiled. "I'm sorry for making it sound like we were forced to take you. We truly are excited to have you. When Jimmie's oldest brother, your grandpa, died, we could not find his daughter. We knew your mother already had a little boy and had just given birth to her second child when she disappeared. The baby was adopted out so quickly no one was able to stop it. Jimmie had heard the stories of your antics around the reservation, but it was after you were with the Smiths that we found out you were Jimmie's niece's son. That's when the tribe decided to bring you home."

"Did you know my mother?" I asked. Some need deep within me was screaming out for that information. Annie continued, "Your mother was having a hard time after your father died and got into serious problems with alcohol. That was when your baby brother was born. Walker, she was almost dead when she was taken to the hospital. It was a miracle she survived! I think deciding to give up her baby was the motivation she needed to get sober. When she was back on her feet, she almost went crazy looking for you. When she couldn't find you, she looked us up and asked us to help her. We did everything we could and finally found out that you had been placed with the Smiths by the LDS Indian Placement program. They were only supposed to keep you during each school year and then send you home for the summers.

"I don't know the whole story, but I heard that when the people from the program went to pick you up, the Smiths wouldn't let you go. I also heard that you refused to go and the people from the tribe couldn't get you to come back with them. I don't know what to think about your refusing to come back. You were only six, and what could you do to stop them from bringing you back? Your mother was on her way to get you when she disappeared again. At the time, Jimmie and I were just married, and we didn't have room for you, so we let you stay with the Smiths."

I asked her if she knew my dad and she replied, "We really didn't know your mom or your dad. We met your mom for the first time when she looked us up. All I know about your dad is that he was killed in a hunting accident. Your mom told me that she had completely quit drinking and had a job. While she was drying out, she said all she could think about was you. She wouldn't have made it if it hadn't been for you. I know you are supposed to be here."

"Why didn't my mom come and get me if she loved me so much?" I asked.

"All I know is that she went to the bus station and never returned. She never picked up the tickets and no one has heard from her since. Rumors started about her going back to drinking, but I will never believe that! I have felt that something terrible happened to her."

We sat there, silently, for quite a while. When she spoke again, she asked me when the agency people were going to bring my things. I smiled and told her I didn't have anything, and besides, I didn't think the agency people wanted to see me again. She told me to get some rest and we would pick up some things tomorrow.

I couldn't go to sleep. All I could do was think about what she had said. Even though my mother had wanted to find me, what gave my aunt and uncle the right to dictate where I was supposed to live? I had asked them to leave me alone. In fact, I had almost begged them to leave me alone. Too much had happened. I knew they would never let me go back home, and I knew what I was going to do about it! I was furious, and I was going to make the Begays regret the day they had ever messed with me! Death by a thousand cuts was my strategy. I would be as good as gold to everyone in the family, but at least twice a week, I would break or destroy something. Once a week I would hurt someone by "accident."

I could see from Walker's eyes that he was a different person when he related this story to me. Perhaps that was why it was so difficult for him to start. He seemed to be possessed by something evil and sinister. So far, everything he had told me about his life just flowed. I loved his life history up to that point and felt connected to him. But now I was starting to dislike not only what I was writing but also Walker himself. He didn't stop to look at me or even to eat. He didn't seem to care about anything but getting through that part of his life story. At that point, I was unable to continue writing because I felt so uncomfortable with what he was telling me. I don't think he even noticed that I had stopped writing. All I know is that I just wanted to leave and not go back.

Walker was talking about how mean one of one of his foster families was to him when he was little and how he had wanted to get even with them for punishing him so severely. He said that his favorite weapon was a screwdriver. He wasn't even in school yet and he used to take electrical and mechanical things apart with the screwdriver and then hide one or two pieces. After that, he would sit there and watch the foster parents go crazy trying to get the thing working, not realizing some of the pieces were missing. Walker said that while he was watching them struggle, he was busy making plans for what he was going to do the next time they punished him. He said he virtually destroyed everything the family owned before they were able to get rid of him. He must have been four or five years old, certainly no more than six, but he said he had them begging for mercy. He stated that this was what he planned to do to his aunt and uncle. I sat, not writing a note, hoping he would recognize this and stop. A voice again echoed through my mind, "Leave if you must, but you are here on My errand." Suddenly, he turned and asked me, "Do you want to know what living with me was like?" "Yes," I said, and began writing again.

On my first day in the Begays' home, which was on the Navajo reservation, I took the boys outside to play ball. I noticed that this area was nothing like where the Smiths' home was located. It was hot, dry, and dirty, and there were old junk cars all over the place. Some of the people lived in homes that looked more like shacks, and others lived in hogans with dirt floors. However, some people like the Begays lived in nice-looking homes that were well maintained.

My first throw was so hard it bruised Tommy's hand through his glove. On the next throw he sidestepped the ball and the ball went through the window. Of course, he tried to blame it on me. The next day, I told them that I would bat some balls to them. This time I got the top pane of the new window, which had just been put in to replace the one that was broken the day before. The following day, just after the other window was repaired, I was in Jack's room looking at his BB gun, and it accidentally went off and shot out the bottom pane of his bedroom window. I wanted to get the top pane too, but I couldn't figure out how without being obvious. I expected the Begays to scream, holler, throw a fit, and maybe even beat me, but all they said was, "Oh honey, you're just accident prone." So I moved on to the toaster. I love toasters! I opened it up and put a plastic lid next to the heating elements. The next time my aunt made toast, the melting plastic not only stunk up the whole house like I wanted, but to my surprise, it started a fire! My aunt went ballistic over that!

I also like freezers. I loosened the nut on the freon and all the gas leaked out. The smell of the toaster was really bad, but compared to the freezer, it was nothing. The smell was so bad it would have gagged a maggot! We ended up having to leave the house for eight days! When we got back, the smell was still so bad that Annie had to burn all the curtains and Jimmie had to repaint the whole house. At that point, I mentioned to them that I had moved the freezer, which might have caused the Freon leak. Jimmie replied, "Don't worry about it, son, we have it under control now."

One day, my uncle decided we needed a break, so he set up a fishing trip. Before we left, I took the fishing tackle box out of the car and put it back in the garage. We got all the way up to Buckeye Lake, in Colorado, and lo and behold, no fishing tackle! Since Uncle Jimmie had to make a trip to the nearest town to buy more tackle, we couldn't fish that day. That night, he put the fishing poles in the backseat of the car with the tips sticking out of the window. Even though the sky was clear, I decided to roll up the windows just in case it rained. The next morning as we prepared to go fishing, we had tackle but no fishing poles because I had "accidently" broken the tips when I rolled up the window. After another trip into town, we had poles and tackle and were ready to fish. The fishing was great! We almost had our limit, but somehow, the stringer didn't get hooked up properly and our nice mess of fish drifted off into the lake. We ended up with the one little fish I had caught just before the stringer malfunction.

The next day, Uncle Jimmie decided to treat us to breakfast in town. When we got to the car we found that the front tire was flat. And of all the luck, so was the spare! Well, that required another trip to town with Jimmie walking and rolling a tire. Long after dark someone brought my uncle back, and wouldn't you know it, the back tire was now flat! We were still one tire short. Once again, Uncle Jimmie had to make another trip to town, and this time with two tires. When he returned he had a brand-new air pump.

The fish were only hitting on Velveeta cheese, but I was hungry, so I decided to make Velveeta cheese sandwiches with lots and lots of cheese, just like Mom used to make. Now we had tackle, poles, and tires, but no bait. By that time, everyone felt that fishing was too stressful, so we went home.

When we got home, the construction people had just finished pouring the cement for our new sidewalk. I'll have to admit they did a beautiful job, but you know how accident-prone I am! I came running around the corner of the house and took a nosedive right into the cement, slipping and falling several times before I could get up. Oh, clumsy me! I was covered from head to toe with cement and was told to go and wash up. Wouldn't you just know it, by morning the cement had set up and they had to tear out the whole job and start over again! Remember when they told me to wash up? Well, as strange as it may sound, some leftover cement somehow made its way into the bathtub drain and it had set up also. Let me tell you, they plunged on that tub until they couldn't plunge anymore. Uncle Jimmie called a plumber, and after he tore up his plumber's snake, they decided to tear out the whole bathtub and replace all the pipes. They were so busy with the bathtub they forgot to check the sink, so the plumber had to make another trip the next day to replace the sink. He brought me a candy bar and some pop and said he wished everyone in town had a teenager like me! Oh well, I think my aunt and uncle had planned on remodeling the bathroom anyway. They were wrapping up the repairs on the sink only to find the window in the bathroom was shattered. I blamed the plumber, but the glass guy smiled and winked at me before going to work.

The next day was Sunday and I would never cause a problem on Sunday because it's a day of rest. Besides, they really needed the rest, and I needed a break! In my evening prayers I asked God what in the world a person has to do to get these people upset? Nobody can be that good and that kind. A voice deep inside of me told me that my aunt and uncle were aware of the pain I was going through and they loved me so much they were willing to be patient and to help me work my way through it.

On Monday, my aunt and uncle brought a medicine man from the tribe to get rid of the evil spirits. If he thought he had dealt with evil spirits in the past, he hadn't seen anything yet! I remembered that Uncle Jimmie had bought a new air pump on our fishing trip, but I realized I couldn't just let the air out of his tires. No, this job would require the use of an ice pick. I poked a hole in the left front and the right rear tires as close to the valve stem as I could. It was really too bad they didn't notice the rear tire until after the front tire had been repaired and the valve stem had been replaced. They couldn't believe their eyes when they found that the rear tire was flat too. By the time they got back with the rear tire, the front tire was flat again because they had changed the valve stem and didn't notice the hole I had poked in the tire.

The medicine man ended up having to buy two new tires, but I wasn't going to let him off that easy. He went to start his car only to find his battery was deader than a door nail. He and Uncle Jimmie went out and bought a new battery only to find out that the battery cable nut had been broken and was not making contact. I've never seen anyone so happy to get out of there as that medicine man was! He didn't even notice the antifreeze and the oil leaks. I had taken the ice pick, put it through the grill, and pounded the pick with a hammer until it pin holed the coils in the radiator, thus causing the leak. Then I loosened the oil filter so it started leaking. In doing so, I noticed that the filter was already loose, so it may not have needed my help. I'm sure he became aware of the leaks before he got home because solid lines of oil and antifreeze trailed his car as he drove away. I think the evil spirits might have gotten to him because I heard, later on, that he got out of the evil spirit business for good.

The Begays never missed church on Sunday, and they prayed every day asking the Lord for mercy. I have to give them credit for hanging in there for over eight months! As often as I could, I found a new way to torment them, and every day they prayed that their bad luck would end. After two toasters, one freezer, a refrigerator, countless windows and doors, new bathroom fixtures, and a destroyed truck engine and transmission, their prayers were answered. I finally ran out of ideas.

I started seeing Mom in my dreams. She would be standing there looking at me with tears in her eyes and saying, "Walker, what have you done? Son, what are you doing?" I started remembering how it was when I was little. I hated what I had done then, but I had done it in self-defense. I hated what I was doing now because these were good people who never intended to hurt me. Looking back, I know that now.

Things in my life were finally starting to settle down. School had started again, and this year, I knew some of the kids, so it was getting easier. I was also gaining a kind of grudging respect for the Begays. Jimmie was what you might call a "teddy bear." He was just a kind and good man. People came to his home at all times of the day and night to get his help with something or another. He was always quick to grab us boys, and we were willing to help anyone who needed it.

There was a lady who lived down the road from us whose husband was a mean drunk. Every time he started drinking, she would come over to the house and stay. Jimmie would wait outside the bar, and when her husband came out, Jimmie would take him home, lock him in the shed, and stay up with him until he sobered up. Jimmie went to work the next day and never complained. As hard as I tried not to, I was starting to admire him.

Annie was everyone's friend. She had a way of spotting someone who was sad or in trouble, and even if she didn't know them, she would go over to them and, within a short time, she would be hugging them and letting them cry on her shoulder. Somehow, she could make everything all right. Sometimes she brought a complete stranger home for a day or two until they could work something out. I have to admit, I loved hugging her. Annie was just slightly on the heavy side, which made for great hugging, if you know what I mean. I was beginning to realize that her kindness and her goodness were getting to me. I liked the way she could tell when things were not quite right with me. She would sit beside me and just talk, not really saying anything, but somehow she made things better. Just like Kathy always had.

The two boys were everyone's best friend; they didn't care if someone was fat, short, tall, ugly, or beautiful. They were friends with everyone. People were drawn to them, and so was I. I felt like I was letting Mom and Dad down because I was starting to really like it there. They had sent me some letters, but I didn't answer them because I didn't know what to say.

School started, and the boys wanted me to try out for the baseball team, but I refused. I only wanted to play for Mom, and I couldn't stand the thought of her not being there at my games. I don't know why, but every time I thought about playing and her not being there, I started crying. Even though I hated it, I couldn't keep from doing it. I'll tell you, I felt like I was being ripped apart from two different directions!

I finally gave in and decided to throw a few balls. Now that I was sixteen, my arm had apparently matured because my first throw was right on the mark. It was so hard it ripped the glove off the catcher's hand. He took two more throws and had to stop because he said I was tearing up his hand. The coach took a couple of my fast balls and then went home to get a sponge to pad his mitt. After that, he caught for me for about an hour. I couldn't help feeling sorry for their pitcher because I knew how he felt. He was going through what I had gone through with the boy from California. My pitching had the coach so excited he started stuttering. I knew I would feel real bad about Mom not being there but I signed up anyway.

That Saturday I spent the whole day pitching into a bucket. My arm was on fire, but I couldn't get my curve ball to break the way I wanted it to. All I needed was practice.

Sunday was church day, so even though I didn't like the church the Begays attended, I went anyway and didn't complain. I felt I owed them at least that much. Their belief was a lot different than mine, and the preacher kept pushing me to get saved. I had a lot of trouble with some of the things he was teaching. I knew the Bible better than he did, so I called him on several things, which, needless to say, was very upsetting to him. I didn't feel good about getting "saved," so I didn't do it.

When I signed up for baseball, one of the questions on the application was, "What religion are you?" Of course I put down The Church of Jesus Christ of Latter-day Saints. Apparently this made it back to the preacher because the following Sunday his sermon was about cults. Dad was a Seventy, which is a special missionary who is authorized to teach nonmembers about baptism, and I had gone with him to a lot of anti-Mormon discussions. The spirit of hate and contention was always there during those gatherings. I was well aware of all the untrue things some preachers were saying about what Mormons believe and don't believe. The most irritating thing I have ever heard is that we don't believe in Jesus Christ! Jesus Christ is the head of our church, and our church is even named after Him! We have the same organization in our church as He did when He was on the earth with prophets, apostles, evangelists, pastors, and teachers for the perfecting of the saints, etc., as stated in Ephesians 4:11-14. All we talk about at our meetings is how to become more like Him by keeping his commandments and living righteous lives.

I knew the Begays' preacher was aiming his preaching at me. I was feeling uncomfortable but didn't know what I could do about it. I noticed that my aunt, uncle, and the boys were feeling the same way. Uncle Jimmie was about halfway to his feet when we heard the words, "Mormons are servants of Satan and are all going to hell." I exploded! I grabbed a song book and ran at the preacher throwing the book at him as hard as I could. I screamed at him that he was a dirty, filthy liar and that all liars are servants of Satan, and he was the one going to hell, not me!

I don't know why, but the tears started flowing and I couldn't make them stop, so I turned around and ran out of the church. I tried to slam the door, but it had one of those things that wouldn't let it slam. I pushed the door shut and then slammed my fist into the glass as hard as I could. The glass didn't break because it was some kind of safety glass, but it shattered. I guess I went crazy because I kept slamming my fist into the glass, over and over, until my hand started bleeding. I had used up every ounce of energy I had and I sank to my knees. I was so drained I couldn't move!

The visions I had received from God were about how to teach the truth to my people, and I had the strongest feeling I was to go back into this church and start fulfilling my calling in life. I could see everything God had shown me flowing before my eyes just like the first time He had shown it to me when I was preparing the talk for Bart's baptism. It was a marvelous vision! I reached for the door handle but never opened the door because I remembered that my battle with God wasn't over yet. I looked up at the heavens and told God, "You should have healed Scotty!"

I got up off my knees, turned around abruptly, and started walking home. My aunt and uncle pulled up beside me in their pickup and asked me to get in, but I refused. The boys got out of the pickup and started walking behind me, not saying a word. They just wanted to be there if I needed them. I was beginning to love those boys. That was my problem; I loved them and hated them at the same time.

When I got home, I went to my room and shut the door. Sometime later, I saw Annie standing at the edge of the doorway. As I looked at her, I could see her face was swollen and her beautiful dark eyes were all red from crying. She pulled me close to her, and through her tears she told me they would never put me through that again. She said I could go to any church I wanted to and they would go with me if I wanted them to. I was surprised when she added, "And that even includes the Mormon Church."

I didn't answer. I just sat there. Then came her sweet voice, "Walker, what can I do to make you happy? What can we do?" I was sorry, but I couldn't think of a single thing to say, so I just sat there. She finally kissed me and left the room. It was at that point I decided it was time to leave. I had to force myself to forget how nice the Begays had been to me and everything they had done for me. All I could think of was that it was time to teach them the ultimate lesson for taking me away from the parents I loved and destroying my life.

CHAPTER 12

KIDNAPPED

I wanted them to feel what it was like to be yanked out of your home and not allowed to go back, so I put together a brilliant plan to get my revenge. I told my aunt that I thought I had broken my fist and asked her to take me to the doctor and have it x-rayed. While we were there, I took one of the kits the doctor used to draw blood and hid it in my coat pocket. I waited for an evening when I knew everyone would be out of the house to make my move. First, I messed up my room to make it look like a struggle had taken place. Then I drew about a pint of blood from my arm and poured it all over the bed and onto the floor. I took what was left and splattered it on the wall. My uncle had a bolo tie of turquoise, which he usually wore, but that night he happened to leave it at home, so I dipped the tip of it into the blood and replaced it in his room. Then I took a pair of his cowboy boots, put them on, and walked through the blood into the bathroom. After leaving one of my shoes by my bed, I grabbed my coat and picked up the food I had stashed. Then I left my aunt and uncle's home, never to return.

As Walker finished this sentence, I stood up and walked away. I went to my tent and started packing my things because I simply couldn't be a party to bringing such evil to light. I was shocked and dismayed to think that Walker would actually frame his uncle for murder just because his uncle cared for him enough to bring him back to his heritage. I found myself muttering as I packed, "How could he do such a thing?" As I completed rolling up my bedroll, I felt a hand on my shoulder. I turned to look at Walker standing behind me. I looked him square in the eyes and said,

"Walker, I can't be your voice. I can't tell people of this ugliness." In a shrill voice, I continued, "Do you realize what you have done?"

"Yes," he said softly, slowly making his way to his knees beside me.

His eyes were no longer full of hate and rage, and I could see that the remorse and regret had returned.

"I told you I wanted them to know how it feels to be snatched from your home and not allowed to return. I wanted to punish not only them but also God and myself. I know now the source of the power I felt. Please continue writing. I need to explain the penalty I paid for doing this disgusting thing. It is necessary for me to tell this part of my story so you understand the lessons I've learned." Walker fell silent and bowed his head.

I just knelt there looking at him for a long time. I couldn't speak. I didn't even know what to say. He had framed his uncle for murder. Finally, Walker looked up at me and said, "If you want to leave and never come back, I'll understand." His look of sadness, desperation, and humility softened my heart.

He began to speak again, this time with the remorse of a lost soul. He said that he had refused to listen to his heart or to have any feelings at all. He didn't pray anymore because he couldn't control his thoughts, and he wouldn't let himself think about his mom and dad because he wasn't going to let anything stop him.

"Uncle Jimmie and Aunt Annie were good people. No matter what I did, they tried to undo it or fix it. They never punished me and almost never raised their voices at me."

He raised his head and stared at me with a look of total desperation.

"They only showed kindness toward me. I had to get out of there, or surrender to them. And I couldn't . . ." He bowed his head again and continued in a voice that made him appear to be deep in prayer.

"Bart had made me promise to make the best out of whatever situation I was in. I broke my promise to him. Now I regret everything I've done and I wonder if they will ever be able to forgive me."

Walker got up and walked to the edge of the mesa where he sat down looking out into space. I watched him for a while. He looked like a thousand lifetimes had pressed him into the bent and withered frame he had become.

I went over and sat down next to him. We sat for a while. "I suppose you and the Savior will have a very interesting discussion when the time comes," I commented casually, staring out at the valley below. "Did you ever attempt to clear your uncle?"

"No" was his answer.

I turned toward him to study his face. "Listen, Walker, I believe I know why I'm here, although that's been tested after hearing how far over the line you've crossed. You talk of the need to get your story out there, but what is this message you have to give? Do you see this as a message for your people?"

"If you mean the Indian tribes, the answer is yes and no," he said. "It's not just for my people, but it's better to be told through them. It is the vision I would have shared if I had taken the peaceful path like Bart wanted me to."

He shifted to find a more comfortable position.

"My story gets worse. I really messed up. But I learned a powerful lesson, and that is that because of the Savior's atonement, there is hope for everyone."

There was simplicity about Walker that made a profound impact when he spoke. I believe that if he had chosen Bart's path, he would have become a great teacher and maybe even a prophet to his people.

"I don't believe I am here by chance, Walker, and I only hope I can do justice to your words. Please let us continue.

Are you ready?"

"Sure," he said and began again like nothing was different. Perhaps he didn't recognize it, but I was different. I didn't allow doubt to sway me again.

After I left, I stayed off the roads, but I made the mistake of not taking water with me. My first thought was that water is heavy, but I quickly realized that water is hard to find when you don't know the country very well. I thought I was going to die of thirst before I made it to Cortez. I had found a lost lamb and a coyote den with four half-grown pups, so I had plenty of food. I had also found some sheep tanks where I got some water, but it wasn't enough to get me through. By the time I reached the outskirts of Cortez, I was crawling on my hands and knees, dragging my backpack and canteen along in the dirt. Luckily, at that point I came to a canal where there was water, but the canal was made of cement and the sides were very steep. I knew that if I got into it I wouldn't be able to get out and would be swept downstream until I came to a gate where I would be drawn under with the undercurrent. So I followed the bank until I came to a hayfield being irrigated. Bart had taught me to take a mouthful of water and to lie on my back and let the water drip into my throat until I could feel my strength come back. Then I could drink all the water I wanted without ill effects. I did exactly that and was soon feeling much better. I was surprised at how quickly my strength returned.

I decided to cross the hayfield to the highway so I could figure out which way to go, but about halfway across the hayfield, I got hit with a swarm of mosquitoes! There must have been a million of them! They got into my eyes, nose, and throat, and they were so thick that I couldn't breathe! I dropped my backpack and canteen and pulled up my shirt putting it over my face. I started running for the edge of the field. When I hit the road, I fell into some deep ruts where a large tractor had been stuck and the bottoms of the ruts were filled with slimy mud. I rolled in it and covered my whole body from head to toe. This did two things: it stopped the mosquitoes and gave me relief from the bites. I retrieved my backpack and canteen and continued on. When I got to the road, I could see the lights of Cortez.

I found the Delores River, but I don't know why I decided to follow it up over the mountains; it was the roughest route I could have taken. The canyon became deep and rugged, so I decided to get up onto the highway. Since the night was dark with no moon, it was very hard to travel. I had gone only a few miles when a van full of people pulled up beside me. They stopped and asked me if I wanted a ride. Before I could say anything, one of the guys asked me if I was an Indian and I told him I was. He said they were up there to make a film about cowgirls and Indians and they needed one more Indian. I told them I didn't know anything about acting, but they said that all they needed was a stand-in and they would tell me what to do. My feet were tired, and I was exhausted from fighting my way through the dark, so I got in. Inside the van, which smelled like burning rags, was an Indian girl who appeared to be drunk. I realized I had made a mistake, and I figured that when they stopped, I would get out. They turned off the highway and drove to an old mining town called Ophir. We were way up in the mountains, but there was an old cabin up there that had a diesel generator for lights. The cabin was full of plants, almost like small trees, that reached up to the ceiling. In the back of the cabin was a fairly large room that had camera equipment and scenery in it. One of the guys offered me a drink of liquor, and I told him that I didn't drink. Then they offered me a cigarette that smelled just like the van had smelled, and I told them I didn't smoke either. At that point, I decided it was time for me to leave. As I pushed my way to the door and forced it open, one of the men grabbed me while another man hit me in the face and knocked me out.

When I came to, I immediately saw what was going on, but I couldn't make any of my muscles move. The most horrible things were happening and all of it was being filmed. They kept shooting some stuff into my arm, and each time it affected me differently. There was a big, heavyset lady dressed in nothing but a cowboy hat and chaps who put me and the Indian girl into disgusting and embarrassing poses. She fondled the girl, beat her, and whipped her with a riding quirt. I don't want to say any more about what was going on. I hope you understand.

I'm not sure how long we were there, but we must have been there for several days. I woke up lying on the floor, naked, with my hands and feet tied, but I realized that I was now at least able to move. My clothes were piled beside me on the floor and I wondered why both my clothes, and the floor, were soaked with blood. I worked my hands into the back pocket of my jeans, and sure enough, my knife was there. As I pulled it out, the blade came open just as it always had. It took a long time to cut the ropes because my hands and feet were tied behind me, but I finally made it. I cut the ropes on my feet free first, only to find I couldn't stand up because my muscles wouldn't work properly. I was hurting everywhere, and I noticed that I was covered with bruises from head to foot.

The Indian girl had her hands and legs tied to the bedposts and she didn't have anything on either. When I was able to get up, I cut her loose but she didn't move. Her eyes were open and I quickly realized she was dead. I tried to close her eyes but they wouldn't close. As I stood there looking at her face, I saw that she was very pretty and very young. The thought came to me then that something like this had happened to my mother. That's why no one could find her after she had gone to buy the bus tickets. I knew I had to get out of there! I struggled to get dressed, but my coat and shoes were missing. I think they hid them to keep me from running off. That didn't matter much to me because, as a small child, shoes hurt my feet, so I rarely wore them anyway. Sometimes I would go all summer and never put shoes on. My feet were calloused and almost like shoe leather.

It took me about an hour to make it out to the highway, and when I got there, I started to run. I'm not even sure which way I was running. The night air was close to freezing, and between the cold and the ten-thousand-foot elevation, I finally collapsed on the road. While falling, I could see lights behind me. It was a truck. The driver stopped, covered me up with a blanket, and put me into the truck. He gave me some coffee, but I spit it out. It tasted horrible! He kept asking me where the wreck was. Because of the bruises on my face and the bloody clothing, the truck driver thought I had been in a car accident and maybe the car had gone over one of the steep cliffs. When I was able to, I told him what had happened to me. I told him about the girl and that she was dead now. He said he knew a deputy sheriff in Naturita and that he would take me there to tell him what had happened. The deputy wasn't home, so we went to the Yellow Rock Café where he ordered me some breakfast. After I ate, he called the sheriff's office in Montrose to report the murder. He put me on the phone, and I gave them all the details I could remember. The phone call ended abruptly because I became seriously ill, vomiting and shaking violently. I was apparently suffering from withdrawals from the drugs they had been pumping into me. The truck driver and a deputy sheriff took me to a doctor's office, in Nucla, and the doctor started working on me. He explained to me that I had become addicted to heroin. He told me that morphine was a substitute, but if I didn't come off the drug slowly, I could die. At that point, I had this overwhelming feeling that I had to get out of there! After the doctor left the room, I decided to make a run for it. I grabbed the morphine he had shown me and put it in my pocket. I thought it would be wise to take a coat, but the only coat I could find was a white lab coat, which I couldn't use because anyone wearing white can be seen a hundred miles away, day or night. The truck driver was in the lobby, and to my surprise, he had bought me some clothes and shoes. I knew that my only chance to get away was to bolt out the back door. He had saved my life, but it surprised me that he was still waiting for me. His name was Chad, and I decided that because of his patience and the love he had shown toward me, I would take his name for my middle name. From then on I called myself Windwalker Chad Smith, although no one knows me by that name.

I left with what I had on. I found a hayloft in a barn to hide in and was able to catch a chicken for food. If I had started a fire they would have found me, so I ate it raw. I don't know how long I stayed there, but I know that I almost died from my reaction to all the drugs I had been given. The morphine helped, but only to keep me from vomiting.

When I was well enough, I went through the trash at a grocery store nearby. I found three blocks of cheese and two cartons of buttermilk. The buttermilk was nasty tasting, but it gave me a lot of energy. I also found three loaves of bread and chocolate-covered doughnuts, which were more like bricks than food. I found a real good coat on someone's clothesline that fit me just fine, and it didn't take long before I was ready to head north to Uravan.

I knew it would take me about a day and a half to get there, and I also knew the stolen morphine might not last that long. Luckily, I was able to make it to a small stream full of squawfish, which dumps into the San Magill River, just a little east of Uravan. Since Bart had taught me how to hand-fish, food was no longer a concern, at least for the time being. My real concern was that I was just about out of morphine. I topped out on the canyon rim on the north side of Uravan, which was located in a deep canyon along the San Magill River. As I sat there on the edge of the sandstone cliff looking down at the town, I could see our house from where I was sitting. I noticed Dad's pickup was still at home, which was unusual, and I wondered what was going on. I wanted to go home so bad it hurt! Near the top of the canyon there was a small abandoned uranium mine where I was able to set up camp before I used the last of the morphine.

About an hour before daylight, I dropped down into the canyon and went to my house. Everyone was asleep, so I decided to go into

Robbie's room first. It was so dark that night I could hardly see him. I didn't realize how much I had missed him! Next, I went to Mom and Dad's room. As I stood there in the doorway, I thought about all the trouble I had caused them. And, on top of that, I was now a drug addict! Right there, I decided I had put my family through enough hell. They didn't deserve to be put through anymore.

I remembered a guy I knew in town named Tim who smoked and drank a lot of beer. He constantly bragged about being able to get anything anyone wanted. He never mentioned drugs, but going to him was my only option. Even though it was early morning, I made my way into town and knocked on his window. He was surprised to see me, but seeing the condition I was in, he invited me in. I asked him if he could help me, and he said he knew a guy that could hook us up. He left me on his bed and slipped out the window. It seemed like hours before he returned. I don't know what he brought me; I only know it made me feel better. As I became more aware, I saw Tim prepare the syringe for himself. I begged him to stop because I couldn't stand the thought of anyone else going through what I was going through. He just looked at me and laughed and was soon higher than a kite! We went back to my cave and were so out of it for a week we were barely aware of our surroundings. The next thing I clearly remember was Tim convulsing from withdrawals in my campsite north of town. Since he had used up all of his money to purchase the drugs, we had no choice but to find a means to pay for more. We decided that the town drugstore was the only chance we had. We put on hooded sweatshirts we had found on a clothesline and walked into the drugstore just before closing. We had our heads covered and pretended we had guns. Tim went behind the drug counter and I took the money from the till. To my surprise he knew what drugs to take and where they were. We were in and out before the police could arrive and were soon back at camp. Since Uravan was a small town and Tim had a reputation for being a troublemaker, we knew it wouldn't take the police long to suspect him. Having burned our bridges there, we decided to head for Grand Junction where Tim's grandfather lived. Tim told me that his grandfather had an attic where we could stay, and since he was drunk all the time, no one would ever know we were there as long as we were careful. It was a long trip to Grand Junction, and we almost starved before we got there. Luckily, my aim with a rock was still great, so we had chipmunks, rabbits, and some grouse to eat.

We entered Tim's grandpa's house to find him passed out on the couch. We set up some beds in the attic where we slept all day. When Grandpa went out at night, we would also leave for the night. I taught Tim how to be invisible so we could go into people's homes and take anything we needed and no one would ever see us. In some of the homes, I sat and watched the people sleep, wondering how it would be to have a life like theirs.

We found some guys who wanted us to get things for them, and to repay us, they gave us the drugs we needed. Since we needed cash for food, Tim decided to muscle out an old man who was shining shoes at the airport. After a week of hard work and hardly any money, we decided we needed to do something different. Grandpa had some handguns in his closet and some ammunition. We needed a big score, so we went after one of our suppliers who Tim knew would have cash and drugs stashed in his house. We entered his house through the back window and surprised our supplier and two other guys who were with him in the room. With the butt of his pistol, Tim struck the closest guy, splitting his head wide open and splattering blood everywhere. He quickly turned his gun on the other two. They both had guns of their own, but I was able to tackle one of them before he could draw his gun, and Tim started beating the third. It was the first time I noticed how ferocious Tim was. There was pure evil in his eyes as he beat the men close to death.

The drugs and money were plentiful, but our hit made it dangerous for us to be seen in public. Unfortunately, it didn't take as long as I thought it would to run through what we took. We talked about making one more hit and then heading for Mexico. Since we needed more than pocket change, we knew we had to hit a bank.

I started watching a bank. It was small and almost never opened on time. The bank tellers were usually not ready for the customers when they showed up, and the bank president came in around noon and left at three. The guard usually didn't put on his weapon and spent most of his time flirting with one of the female tellers as well as helping the old ladies. I tell you, that guard must have been really hard up because the teller was one ugly woman! One night they even forgot to shut the vault. I told Tim that bank was begging to be robbed.

Our bank job went like this. When they opened, we were the first ones through the door. The guard was there, but he didn't have a gun. We immediately headed for the break room where the tellers were finishing their morning coffee. Tim held a gun while I used electrical tape to tie and gag everyone. We took the guard to the break room and tied and gagged him. Then we locked the doors but left the blinds open so we could see anyone approaching the bank. We found a lot of bags full of money, so we took two huge bags; we went out the back door and hid in a dumpster. We stayed in that awful, smelly dumpster for three days until activity died down and we were able to escape. Of course, we had made sure that the trash wasn't going to be collected on any of those three days! The bags were really heavy and it was hard getting them back to the attic. It appeared that we were invisible because no one even noticed us.

Only later did we find out that the Fed was using this bank for temporary storage. We didn't have time to take all the money pouches, and by dumb luck, we happened to grab the pouches of old money, which were going to be returned to the Fed to be destroyed. That money had no recorded serial numbers. If we had stolen the pouches of new Fed money that had recorded serial numbers, they would have been able to track us. Because none of the new Fed money had been touched, the police investigation deemed it an inside job.

We had a real problem. The bags of money were extremely heavy, and there was no way we could carry the money and walk to Mexico. Tim's grandpa, who lived close to the Colorado River, had an old pickup he used about once a year to haul trash, and we decided to take it thinking that he wouldn't miss it for a long time. When we tried to start the engine, we discovered the battery was dead. So we got the keys to Grandpa's car and hooked the car up to the front of the pickup, which was located in an area of pasture a short ways from the river. I told Tim to start driving the car, and when the pickup started, I would honk the horn so he could stop the car and unhook it. When the pickup started I honked the horn, but lo and behold, the horn didn't work!

I waved at Tim to stop the car, but he thought I wanted him to go faster. We were now heading toward the river. I pushed on the brakes as hard as I could but to no avail. I thought for sure he would stop when he got to the river, but to my surprise, he made a U-turn just before he got to the water's edge and went speeding off again. I tried flashing my lights, but there was so much dust and sand he didn't notice. When he got to the end of the pasture, he made another U–turn, and this time the pickup bounced on two wheels. I could picture myself rolling over and over, but somehow we made it. We were really flying. I was feeling desperate by then and wondering how in heaven's name I was going to get the crazy fool to stop.

Once again heading toward the river I could see that Tim was about to negotiate yet another U- turn, but this time I was able to get the pickup into first gear. I locked the brakes and crimped the wheels to the right. As luck would have it, Tim got too close to the river, and the car's wheels started spinning in the sand which high-centered the car. He was sitting there with the engine going wide open, sand and gravel going everywhere, with the smell of burning rubber filling the air.

I walked up to the car and knocked on the window. As Tim rolled the widow down, I could see the speedometer on 120 mph. He looked at me and asked, "What are you doing out there?" I reached in, turned the motor off, and took the keys. I told him he had to get off the stuff he was taking because he was going to kill someone. I also told him I didn't want to ride with him to Mexico. We went over to a nearby cottonwood tree and sat there looking at the car realizing we had a huge amount of money and no way to get it to Mexico. I told Tim I thought we should give ourselves up and see if we couldn't get off the drugs and maybe make a life for ourselves. He didn't look at me but said he thought I had a good idea. Then Tim got up and started to walk away. Suddenly, he spun around with his gun in his hand and fired point-blank into my face! The bullet ripped through my hair and the gun powder burned my face and eyes.

I instantly drew my gun and gave him a double tap in the chest. He was dead before he hit the ground. I can still see the crazy wild look in his eyes as the bullets hit him. My left eye had swollen up so badly that I thought my eyeball was going to pop out of my head. I finally lanced it with my knife to relieve some of the swelling. That's why I am almost totally blind in that eye.

I decided to run, and once again I left without a coat. I knew I couldn't stay in Grand Junction and I had nowhere left to go. Then I remembered these mesas and my home in Uravan. It took me almost a month to make it back to my campsite at the abandoned mine, and when I got there, I made a commitment that I would never do drugs again.

As I sat there at my campsite, my thoughts took me back to what I had gone through to get home. I remember lying in a culvert beneath the highway, vomiting and sweating profusely for days as I went through acute withdrawal brought on by the lack of drugs. I thought I was going to die over and over, and honestly, I wished I could have. When I came to my senses, I noticed I was sharing the culvert with some rattlesnakes. They came into the culvert in the evenings because it had been warmed by the sun and they liked the warmth. Even though I was shaking violently and heaving my guts out, they didn't seem to notice me. I guess I was still invisible. I was weak and hungry and desperately needed food, so that night I asked brother snake to give his life to save mine. When I awoke in the morning, all the snakes were in the culvert but one. It was outside the culvert on the sand, stretched out almost straight, with his head on a large rock. I picked up a large rock and crushed his head. The Spirit whispered to me to peel the skin back carefully and not to tear it because I could use it to carry the water I would need for my travels. After almost dying of thirst on my trip from Arizona to Colorado, I was ready to listen. People say rattlesnake tastes like chicken, but obviously they have never tasted rattlesnake. It actually has the same texture and taste as fresh salmon. I felt like I needed to thank God for brother snake and his sacrifice, so I did. This was the first time I had prayed since I was taken from my home, and Bishop, the strangest thing happened; I felt the Savior's hand on my shoulder. I fell to the ground with my eyes closed and saw myself kneeling down kissing his feet. I saw the nail prints as I bathed his feet with my tears. When I woke up from that dream, or vision, I committed to never stop praying again. That was when I realized that the only man-made things in heaven are the scars in the Savior's hands, feet, and side.

During my journey home I lived on rabbits, chipmunks, grouse, and an occasional snake. I was as low as a man can get, but as I neared the canyon edge that overlooked Uravan, the sense of home filled me with a peace I had not felt since Bart's baptism. I began to remember all the things Mom and Dad had taught me about our Heavenly Father and His forgiveness. I sat at the edge of the canyon rim most of the night basking in the warmth radiating from my home.

I waited until early morning, and while it was still dark, I dropped down into the canyon. I decided to go to the house. No one ever locked their doors in Uravan, and our house was no exception. The first thing I did was to go into my room. Everything was just as I had left it. The eagle feather and pouch were still right there by my bed. I wanted to take them, so I did. I needed the lessons they had to teach me and the record of the visions I had received that I had put into my pouch for safekeeping. I also knew this would be a good way to let my family know I had been there and that I was still alive. Next, I went to Robbie's room where he appeared to be sleeping soundly. I couldn't believe how much he had changed since the last time I'd seen him. I stood there looking at him for a long time, the pain in my chest making me realize how much I loved my family and how much I missed them. I went into Mom and Dad's room, and this was where my heart really broke! The room was dimly lit by the full moon, and I noticed something lying between Mom and Dad. I leaned over and looked closer. To my surprise it was a baby! Mom finally had her baby girl! At that moment, she rose up and looked right at me. I was startled, but I could see that she wasn't totally awake. She said, "Walker, are you okay?" "Yes, Mom," was my reply. "Walker, what have you done?" she asked. "Things I can't change," I answered. "You can always make things right." She laid her head back down on the pillow and was sound asleep again. I stood there looking at her for the longest time. I realized that I had forgotten how truly beautiful she was. I left the house, climbed back up the canyon, and headed to my campsite. I gathered what little I had and made my way to these mesas.

Oh, by the way, somewhere hidden in the attic of that old white house by the river in Grand Junction, there's a fortune waiting to be found. I didn't take any of it with me when I left.

CHAPTER 13

FINDING THE ANSWERS TO ALL THINGS

Walker stopped talking and stared out at the valley before us. "How long have you been here on the mesas?" I asked. By his appearance, my guess would have been somewhere between twenty or thirty years!

"Three years," he said.

"Three years? Then that would make you around twenty years old!" "I'm actually nineteen, almost twenty," said Walker.

His response left me in shocked amazement. The disease Walker had contracted had ravished his body and had made him appear to be well beyond his actual years. However, he had managed to subsist quite well on the mesas. He had no need for money because he had gleaned from what nature provides.

When I first arrived, he showed me some large pack rat nests throughout the rocks. He had found a lot of food there like pinion nuts and seeds and so on. He told me that if a rat stores it, it will be safe to eat. Also, he is deadly with a slingshot when hunting wild turkey and grouse. He stored his meat in burlap sacks and placed them in the cold, dark cavities in the rocks. He called the deep cracks in the rock "crevices." The air flow through the crevices is very cold in the winter and remains cool during the summer. To prevent spoilage, he had smoked about half of what he had hunted. As he walked me through his setup on the mesas, Walker explained to me that he got most of his meat during hunting season. Deer like to feed in the hayfields at Spring Creek Ranch, which is about ten miles to the north. In hunting season, the hunters will shoot a deer late in the evening and then not be able to find it. They follow the blood trail to where the blood stops and then they stop tracking. In most cases the deer has just about run out of blood and dies fifty to one hundred yards from where the blood trail ends.

On the nights when the moon was full, Walker would track down a deer the hunters were unable to find, dress it out, and then take it back to his camp. He was usually able to get four to five deer during the season. The way he mixed the meat with seeds, nuts, and honey was a clever way to make his meat go a long, long way, and it was very nutritious. When the hunting was poor, there were rabbits, prairie dogs, and pack rats to live on.

As we walked around the mesas, Walker pointed out some lodge pole pine, each about fifteen feet long, stacked by a pool of water. This pool was quite deep and only about nine or ten feet across. Someone else must have brought the poles here because there was no lodge pole pine in the general area. In the winter when it started freezing, he would slide the base of the poles into the water using the bank as a fulcrum. When the ice was completely frozen, he put rocks into a homemade sling he had fashioned on the elevated end of the poles. When he had put enough rocks into the sling, the lever action lifted the near side of the ice up about eighteen inches. The far side of the ice remained in the water. Walker would then fill in the gap between the ice and the water's edge with rocks and sand, making it airtight. The layer of ice acted as insulation, so the remaining water in the pool didn't freeze. He used an old coffee can and a leather rope to draw water, like you would draw water from a well. This gave him access to water in the winter without having to continually break the ice.

Walker rose from his perch on the edge of the mesa, brushed off the pain, as if dusting himself off, and made his way to his lean-to. As I watched him walk away from me, it occurred to me that each time I see his profile, I'm looking at a different man. For the first time, I was picturing him as a twenty-year-old barefoot Hopi warrior clad in just a breach clout. He told me that he usually wears a breach clout in the summer, but when I showed up, he put on the clothes he had come up there with because he was raised to be modest. He had tried to tan leather but hadn't mastered the technique. When I first arrived, he was chewing on a piece of deer hide to soften it. He asked for my assistance, but I politely declined.

There is so much to discover with Walker. I continued to watch this modest, brave, and strong young man as he walked away from me toward his lean-to. I have been calling it a lean-to, but in actuality it is more of *a cave. A large slab of sandstone had broken away from a sandstone wall and had fallen against another large boulder creating a cavity open on both ends. I don't know whether he walled up the back entrance or whether it was already covered when he got here. He covered the front entrance with several deer hides he had dried in the sun, folding them back to create a doorway large enough to walk through easily. When it is really cold in the winter, he walls up the majority of the opening with rocks. He said that with a small fire, he can easily keep warm, and he has made himself quite comfortable here.*

The swarm of thoughts created by his retreating profile was suddenly broken by a coughing spell. I'm not sure what disease could age a young man so brutally, but I have read about something going around in California that attacks the immune system. It depletes people until they waste away to a shadow of their former selves and end up dying from diseases the immune system can't handle. As far as I know, there is no cure. We talked about it several days ago during one of our meals together, and I strongly suggested he come with me to see a doctor. He politely declined, reminding me of my mission here with him. He then changed the subject.

I found myself alone with my thoughts as the sun dipped below the horizon casting long shadows over the valley.

Suddenly, I was startled by a voice. "Tomorrow is the last day of his mortal existence," the voice said. I looked over, and sitting beside me was a man looking like the young warrior I had imagined Walker once was.

"Please, don't be afraid," he said. "I am here to answer the question you have in your mind. You have been sent here to witness and record. I have been sent here to clarify and prepare."

"Who are you?" I asked.

"My name is Aaron, and I am a messenger sent from God to prepare Walker to make his final journey. Your worthiness has allowed me to visit with you and advise you of the coming event." He stood without effort, well-being radiating from him. "Please, follow me."

Instantly, I was in front of the lean-to peering in at the sleeping Walker. A dog was lying at his feet. "Scotty is also here to escort Walker. His loyalty and love have made him the perfect companion for the journey."

I started to ask him what I could do to assist in Walker's comfort, but before I could summon the words, Aaron spoke, "You will know what to do when the time is right. What do you really want to know?"

"Why me?" The words escaped my lips before I could measure their impact on my soul. Aaron laughed. "Are you so unsure of yourself that you didn't recognize the spirit directing you here?" His smile brightened the sky, and his eyes humbled me to my knees. I bowed my head in reverence.

"Your purpose for being here goes far beyond the recording of Walker's words. You have been called of God and foreordained to carry on where Walker will leave off. You are here because you were willing to answer the call." I knew, instantly, that his words were true and that I had a special work to perform.

"Bishop, when you arise in the morning, ask Walker to accept baptism. He may speak of unworthiness, but you know the Lord has forgiven him. If he asks about Tim, tell him he will be able to go into the Spirit Prison, where Walker knows the unrighteous spirits go when they leave this earth, to assist in teaching him the Gospel of Jesus Christ. If Tim accepts the teachings, Walker will be able to be his guide and answer questions about the Spirit Prison and how he can enter Paradise where the righteous reside. Yes, Tim's mother is a Mormon, and Walker will also be the answer to her many prayers over the years. Walker is ready." I looked up to gaze upon him, but he was gone. I found myself lying on my back with my feet hanging over the edge of the cliff staring into the heavens. The stars were infinite.

I awoke in the morning to find Walker sitting at the edge of the cliff watching the color return to make day.

Without speaking, I sat beside him with paper and pen in hand.

"Bishop, I find my mind weighed down with concerns for my uncle and his family. Before you woke up I almost left to go visit him. I'm sorry, but if it weren't for the dream I had last night, I would be gone this morning."

"Please, tell me about your dream, Walker," I said.

It was an amazing dream! I was aware of everything around me, as if I were awake. At first, you were standing over me with someone I didn't recognize but who I instantly knew. Next, I was standing there looking at you when I felt something brush my leg. I looked down to see Scotty, and my eyes watered as I bent down and felt his love for me. My mind was filled with so many questions. I wanted to know why God didn't heal Scotty. Before I had asked the question, the answer was given to me, "Because time is measured unto man and unto beast." The man with you was surrounded by bright light that appeared to be brighter than the sun. Before I could ask my next question, he answered, "Yes, Walker, I am a messenger from Heavenly Father and my name is Aaron. What is it you seek?" I could feel his love and kindness flowing into me.

Aaron motioned to his right and said, "Look," and I looked where he was pointing. I could see my whole journey with Scotty including my throwing the rock at him, the black dog, and so on, right up to the point where I knelt down in the reception room and called upon God to heal him. I promised God I would never be bad or sin again.

Aaron, wanting me to understand how impossible this promise would have been for me to keep, said, "Look." I could see the Savior as a baby. I noticed that darkness seemed to surround him. The darkness stayed at a distance at first, but as He got older, it began to close in on Him. He was being tempted continually to sin, but he resisted all the temptations. I knew that if he had sinned just one time, He wouldn't have been able to be our Savior. I watched his life and saw that he never got any relief, peace, or rest because of the darkness.

"Look." And I looked. The Savior was in the Garden and I saw that He was suffering horribly and He was bleeding from every pore of His body. I felt the pain He was going through, but I couldn't really comprehend it. In my mind the suffering in the Garden was mild compared to what He suffered all of his life to remain sinless. I had a full understanding that He never allowed the darkness to overtake Him so that he could be a sinless sacrifice for my sins and the sins of all mankind.

I looked toward Aaron, and a personage of glory far beyond all description was standing there with him. I knew immediately that it was Jesus. He took me in his arms and I started crying. I told Jesus, "Thank you for loving us so much and for being willing to go through all that suffering to keep the promise you made to your Father. I could never have kept the promise I made that day with Scotty. Please forgive me," I said as I sank to my knees, crying uncontrollably.

The next thing I remember was Aaron putting his hands on my shoulder and lifting me to my feet. He said, "Look," and as I looked, I could see a man and a woman training four dogs to hunt cougars. Part of their training was to teach the dogs to attack viciously.

"Look." And I saw the lady pulling me from under the dogs and taking me to the doctor. While she was helping the doctor work on Scotty, she was begging and pleading for God to let Scotty live. God granted her prayer or Scotty would have died on the table.

"Look," Aaron said again. I could see the couple tearing down the kennels and taking their dogs to good homes. They loved dogs and had owned many in their lifetime, but they never again taught any of them to fight.

It excited me to know that the angel could show me such things, and my mind was filled with questions. "Will the bishop tell my mom and dad what happened to me?" He said, "Look." I looked and I could see myself standing by Mom's bed, and in a quiet voice, telling her what had happened to me. I could hear her thoughts telling me she had been assured that I would be okay. "I am glad you are in God's hands," she thought. "Thank you for telling us about the baby. We had almost stopped trying to have any more children. She is a beautiful baby girl, and we will teach her about you and she will love you."

Once more, Aaron said, "Look." I could see the people from the agency picking me up and I could see four heavenly personages in the room with us. They were clean and pure messengers who appeared to have great power and authority.

"Look."

I could see Mom mentally screaming at God. One of the personages was receiving Mom's message and relaying it to God. Another was giving me instructions on what she would like me to say. The four personages moved close to Dad with heads bowed as if in prayer. When I looked at Dad, a dark mist was covering him. The one standing by Mom bowed his head. At that instant, Dad decided to make his move. All four of the personages screamed at me, "Do it, do it now!" When

I laid my hands on his head, the dark mist faded away. As I walked toward the door with the agency people, Dad's emotions drained out of him.

Again, Aaron said, "Look." I looked, and as the door shut, Dad sprang to his feet, flew into the bedroom, and grabbed the gun, which was always loaded. He was in a dead run when he entered the living room. One of the messengers blocked his path and he suddenly stopped. He dropped to his knees just before he reached the closed door, looked up to heaven, and cried, "Oh God, I can't do this anymore! Please let me go after him. Please don't let them take my son. Take my life, please take my life, but don't take my son!" Mom picked up the gun and unloaded it. Aaron told me that my dad had to go through this experience so he could get a better understanding of the power of the Atonement. "Look." I looked again and could see the Savior being taken out of the Garden of Gethsemane by the soldiers. Dad's pain from having me taken away was giving him an understanding of the pain Heavenly Father felt as his Son was being led away to atone for the sins of mankind.

Aaron said, "Look." I looked and I could see Dad in a mist of darkness. As I looked into the darkness, I could see horrible scenes of war. On the other side of the darkness I saw our family. When Dad returned to our family, the darkness was still in his mind. I could see the scenes of war going over and over in his mind at night. And I could see Robbie and I sitting in his lap until the scenes went away and he calmed down. It was destroying him physically and spiritually. "Look." I looked and I could see him falling to his knees and refusing to allow the war to have any more power in his life.

Then I could see the Savior emerge from the tomb with a large bowl in His hands and go to Dad.

I saw Dad putting something into the bowl.

As Dad put things into the bowl, I could see him change. By the time he was done, his countenance shone like the angel's. I realized that the bowl was a symbolic representation of where a person's sins go when he repents and gives them to Jesus. Jesus turned and walked a short distance toward an ocean, and when he reached it, he knelt down and emptied the bowl. I knew that my dad's sins had been forgiven through the blood of the Lamb and placed into the Sea of Forgetfulness, never to be mentioned again.

Aaron asked, "Do you know the meaning of these things?" I told him I knew of my dad's love for me and I knew of the Savior's love for my dad. I also knew that my dad's sins had been forgiven and that he had been healed from what he had done in the war. I understood that he would never again suffer because of what he had to do to protect our freedom, but I still didn't know the meaning of all these things.

Aaron said, "In your dad's heart was written gentleness, kindness, respect for all mankind, and a love of freedom for himself and his family. The things he had to do in the war made him violently ill sometimes for weeks at a time. It was so against his true nature it was destroying his body as well as his spirit. Do you want to see your dad's true nature?"

"Yes," I said.

As I continued to watch, I could see Dad and Brother Connor searching everywhere for someone. They had to go deep into the dark mist, so it was hard to see what they were doing. I could see someone lying on the ground. It was Bear Hunter; he could not get over what he had done to us little boys. His wife and child had left him, and in despair, he had turned to alcohol. He was on the edge of total destruction. Dad and Brother Connor put him in Brother Connor's plane and flew him to a big building where people were waiting to take care of him. I could see Mom, Dad, and the Connors making many visits to see Mr. Hunter. Finally, I could see Mr. Hunter, clean and sober, working for Dad in the mines.

"This is your dad's true nature," said Aaron.

"Look," Aaron said again, and I could see the Savior teaching the parable of the Good Samaritan to a large crowd. I was able to visualize the Samaritan paying the innkeeper to provide lodging and care for the man who had been robbed and beaten.

Then I heard the Lord say, "The King will reply, 'Truly I tell you, whatever you did for one of the least of these brothers and sisters of mine, you did for me.' (Matthew 25:40).

I said, "Now I understand the meaning! As for the horrible things he had to do in the war, Dad had to understand he was in a battle of good against evil. The Savior will do this for anyone who repents." And for the first time, I knew that there was hope for me.

Walker," Aaron said, "Kathy tried to help him overcome his problems, but she couldn't do it. His love for you was the only thing that could have broken him down to the point where he could be healed."

I told Aaron, "I would gladly go through every second of the pain I have passed through again, just to be able to see the change in my dad and to know he would never have any more nightmares."

Aaron put his arm around my shoulder and said, "I know you would."

The angel asked me to look again, and I saw that four personages were in the room. They were the four babies Mom had given birth to but who had not lived. Because they were valiant and pure spirits, they didn't have to be tried and tested here on the earth. They only needed mortal bodies to go back into the presence of Heavenly Father from whence they came. Because of Mom's goodness and her great faith, she was given the privilege of providing bodies for these special spirits. I then saw a girl who was close to Mom. The angel explained that she was the baby that would come. She would be the joy and the reward for all of Mom's prayers and for her exercising such great faith."

I saw that Walker had tears rolling down his cheeks. He paused for several minutes, and we savored the joy of knowing his father had been healed. I decided that now was a good time to tell Walker of my experience with Aaron, but before I could speak, he continued with his dream.

Now my mind hungered to know more. I realized I could have the answer to any question I had ever had in my life. My thought was, how can God make all things work for the good of those who love Him?

Aaron said, "Look." I looked and could see a lady about Mom's age who was dressed like those in ancient times. She was on her knees praying to Heavenly Father for a child. Her prayers flowed into two golden boxes. The first box, marked Prayers Uttered, filled quickly and was taken to the Lord each time it was filled. The second box filled up much more slowly. Labeled Diligence, Trust, and Faith, this box was also delivered to the Lord when filled. I saw that a little baby boy was sent to a woman named Hannah because she had made a vow that the Lord accepted, filling the second box. The child's name was Samuel, which means "Because I have asked him of the Lord." This was the prophet, Samuel, of the Old Testament.

"Look." I looked and I could see a husband and wife. I saw the wife working behind a counter at a store. A black van full of people drove up to the front door. A man got out, walked through the door, and shot her in the stomach. He took the money, liquor, and cigarettes from the store and left. The woman lived, but her injuries had left her unable to have children. For years they filled box after box marked Prayers Uttered. I witnessed them also filling many boxes marked Diligence, Trust, and Faith.

"Look." I looked and could see a much younger single mother with two young children driving late at night and dozing off; she was shaking her head and trying to keep awake while driving. I could see a heavenly messenger whispering to her that she should pull over and rest. He made the same request a number of times but got the same response. I didn't have to look because I knew what was going to happen.

"You must look," said Aaron. Even though I didn't want to look, I obeyed. I witnessed the woman from behind the counter in the store come upon the scene of the accident and I watched as she nursed the young woman and then took her and her children to the hospital. She held the younger woman's hand as the younger woman passed into the next world. Then I was in a courtroom with the husband and wife and the deceased woman's two small children. In the back of the room was the young single mother who had passed on and her grandfather who was the angel who had whispered to her in the car before the accident. Sitting close to them was Mr. Shoemaker, a.k.a Fat Man, and the young lady who was in the backseat of the car when they took me from my home. I could see the relief in the young single mother's face as the judge stated, "Adoption granted." The young mother knew then that the two babies she loved so much would now have a complete family and would be loved and cared for all their lives. Mr. Shoemaker and the young lady quietly got up and left the courtroom feeling great satisfaction for what they had accomplished. Both the wife and the young single mother were in desperate need, and each woman was the only one who could answer the prayers of the other.

Aaron asked, "Knoweth thou the meaning of this?"

I looked into his countenance and replied, "I know prayers are all taken to God and He doesn't miss any. I know He answers all prayers. I know He will never give us anything or do anything that will harm us or keep us from returning to Him. However, I don't know the meaning of everything I have just seen."

Aaron smiled and said, "Do you know that God did not shoot the lady who prayed with all of her heart to have children?"

"Yes, it was the man in the van," I said.

"Do you know that God did not make the young lady fall asleep?"
"Yes, I know He tried to warn her, but she wouldn't listen."

"The Father knows the beginning from the end, and He directs all things for those who exercise faith with diligence, placing their trust solely in Him for their own good."

"Look." I now recognized the road and the black van stopping and backing up. There was a heavenly messenger standing by me telling me not to get into the van, but I didn't pay attention. Then I saw myself lying on the floor of the cabin. The entire floor was covered with sheets of plastic. The Indian girl was on the bed, and one of the younger men who had been in the van was trying to get her loose. They had given me an animal tranquilizer, which paralyzed my muscles so I was conscious but couldn't move. The room burst with activity, and everyone was screaming at the young man telling him he was going to cause them to get caught. The older brother of the young man stepped forward. He was tall and blond, but his soul was black; he was the one who had shot the woman in the store so callously. He went over to the camera and turned it on. He then stooped down and cut his younger brother's throat. After committing that evil act, he moved to the camera and continued filming while the others began beating and cutting his brother as he lay on the floor dying.

Aaron quoted, "Therefore doth my Father love me, because I lay down my life that I might take it up again. There is no greater way to show love than to be willing to give your life to save another." "Look." I looked and could see the young man struggling to get to me. With his last breath he put my knife in my back pocket. They had tied my feet and started to tie my hands in front of me, but the fat lady with the hat told them to tie my hands in the back so I couldn't use them as a weapon.

Then I was standing over that young, beautiful girl watching her soul leave her broken body. Standing beside me was the messenger who whispered to me, "Your mother is dead and that is why she never came to pick you up; she fought to her last breath." I became aware of an old junk car among other junk cars that had been abandoned on the reservation; her body was still in the trunk.

I turned to Aaron and asked, "What happened to the man with the black soul?"

"Look." I looked again and I saw police all over the place. They had the camera equipment, guns, pills, and a large truckload of plants. The sheriff was from Montrose County, not San Magill. I saw arrests being made in five states as well as in Mexico, Hong Kong, and Singapore. The bigge st arrest came when the deputy sheriff arrested the Telluride business owner, who was also the mayor of Telluride, as he stepped off his plane.

"Look." I was standing, holding the hand of the beautiful girl, along with more than a dozen other young people, and out of the dark mist came the six who had tortured or killed each of us. They were skin and bones and hideous-looking except the one who had given me the knife. They looked at all of us and witnessed for themselves what they had done to us. Aaron quoted Job, "The heavens shall reveal his iniquity; and the earth shall rise up against him." There was a great moan coming from Mother Earth, crying for justice for the innocent blood that these six had spilt on her. Five shrank to the ground and slinked off into the darkness. The young man who gave me the knife was asked to remain. I walked over and put my arm around him and told the others what he had done for me. They received him like a hero.

Aaron said, "Do you know the meaning of what you have seen?"

"I know about repentance, but is justice served by bringing the young man out of the darkness?" "Look, again." I could see records kept in heaven. The records in heaven were mostly what we did on earth according to the commandments of Jesus. I saw a large book with the title *Book of Life* with chapter headings in it such as "Prayers Uttered," "Faith," "Baptism," and "Following the Direction of the Holy Ghost." I understood that heavenly beings are appointed to write down all of the thoughts, words, and deeds of those on the earth. "When you repent of sin, it is erased from the book."

Aaron said, "Look." I looked and saw that one of the records was my *Book of Life*. I could see that my life was also recorded in the records of everyone I have ever known and everyone with whom I have come into contact.

"Look." I looked and could see all those who had committed horrible sins. They were required to stand before those they harmed. No fancy words, devious plans, or lies because their lives were what they were and were illustrated in their life books. Even Mother Earth will testify against them.

Aaron spoke. "Because Jesus was tempted, suffered for all of our sins, and knows all things, He will judge us. If we deserve mercy, He will act in our behalf. He takes into consideration all the circumstances and influences surrounding our lives. He, and only He, is qualified to be our Deliverer, Mediator, Counselor, and Redeemer. Because He laid down his life for us, we are able to take advantage of His mercy and have justice satisfied."

I told the angel I had been taught of mercy and justice but had not understood how it all worked.

Aaron turned to me and said, "Our night together is almost at an end. You have one more question, ask, and you shall receive." My desire was to know why sometimes bad children come from good families.

"Look." I looked and I saw a wonderful family whose parents had great faith in God. They were wonderful mentors to their children. They taught them about God and how to pray to Him. The oldest and the youngest children were rebellious from birth, while the middle two were obedient and a delight to their parents. The oldest and youngest started down the same path together; the path was filled with evil. No light could penetrate the darkness. I recognized these two as the brothers from the black van.

"Look." I looked as the family knelt together and filled many boxes with their prayers. Many others also prayed for these two. As the boxes filled, they were delivered to God who sent messengers to warn and to try to guide the two boys. The older boy would not listen to the guidance of the messengers. Even so, the messengers did not stop trying to help him. On the other hand, the younger brother finally did listen to the voices of the messengers. After pleading with his brother to change, he decided to leave. The older brother and his evil friends wouldn't let him go. He begged God for help. When the older brother was torturing the beautiful Indian girl, he decided he wouldn't let them kill her as they had done to the others. He knowingly gave his life to save the girl, and me, because he recognized the evil.

"Knowest thou the meaning of this?"

"I know the power of love and the power of prayer, and I know that God never gives up on us. I know He will do all He can to help guide us but will never take away our right to choose who we are and what we will become. I think I'm beginning to understand the visions!"

The angel quoted Jeremiah, the son of Hilkiah, "Before I formed thee in the belly I knew thee; and before thou camest forth out of the womb I sanctified thee, and I ordained thee a prophet unto the nations." He continued, "God knows all his children, both good and bad. He gives each of His children the greatest opportunity to succeed and return to Him. Some of the best families receive the most rebellious spirits because this is their only chance to make it. Heavenly Father knows what He is doing. Because of the teaching of these good families He is able to save many of the rebellious children when they are old. Heavenly Father's Plan of Salvation is able to provide everyone with the chance to choose if they are willing to do what it takes to return to his presence."

Aaron turned and embraced me. "God knows your heart. Your journey on the earth will soon be completed. I have been asked to be your guide and messenger in your last days here. Now awake and have Bishop write your vision." With those words I woke up.

Walker fell silent, reflecting again on the visions and words taught to him during the night. His description of the dream reminded me of 1 Corinthians 13:12, which says, "For now we see through a glass darkly; but then face to face: now I know in part; but then shall I know even as also I am known." We sat silently for a time, staring again out into the valley.

"Walker," I finally said, "I spoke with Aaron as well." He looked up at me, eager to learn what Aaron had told me. "He asked me to talk to you about something."

"Before you continue, Bishop, am I worthy to be baptized?"

I shouldn't have been surprised at the question, but somehow I was. "How did you know the angel wanted me to ask you to be baptized?"

"I didn't. When I saw the forgiveness of the young brother, I realized that perhaps I could be forgiven as well." We both took the time to clean up and don our best clothes. We started with a prayer, and I said a few words.

"Train up a child in the way he should go: and when he is old, he will not depart from it." This is a quote that speaks directly to your situation. You have been raised by good people who taught you to fear God and taught you to recognize good from evil. It is time to cleanse you from the evil that has followed you and tried to destroy you." We waded into one of the pools, and I raised my arm to the square. I could see Aaron, who had authorized the baptism, and two other angles who were acting as witnesses. I said, "Windwalker Chad Smith, having been commissioned of Jesus Christ, I baptize you in the name of the Father, and of the Son, and of the Holy Ghost. Amen." At this point, I completely immersed Walker in the water and brought him up out of the water, symbolizing his death in the flesh and rebirth in the spirit as a pure and clean son of God. I hate to admit it, but at that point I was almost envious because he was totally clean and sinless. I knew he was going to die either tonight or tomorrow and that he would be taken straight to Paradise where the Savior would be waiting for him.

At dusk we retreated again to the side of the cliff. "I want to continue writing, but I am out of paper. I know it's getting late, but I will leave right now and get back as soon as I can. Are you going to be okay?" As always, his answer was, "I'll be fine." But I could see in his face that he wasn't fine. I knew that if I left, I may not return in time to be present when he passed on, as Aaron had prophesied. I left the mesa in a dead run. In doing so, I almost fell as I descended the crevasses, which were the only way of getting off the mesa.

CHAPTER 14

REDEMPTION

I hit the ground running. It was getting dark and I had over ten miles to cover. I ran until I thought my chest was going to burst, and then fell to my knees and begged God to give me strength. I knew that God does not lie; this was Walker's last day. I felt like one of the unwise virgins without enough oil to await the coming of the bridegroom. My only hope was that God would give me my second wind. I returned to my feet, and thankfully he gave it to me. I continued on my desperate journey.

As I climbed out of the valley Walker and I had spent days observing, I knew I still had two miles to go to reach my car. Darkness had enveloped me, leaving me without a good trail to follow and no way to distinguish the direction I must go. I found myself brushing by cactus and sage, which tore at my flesh and caused me to stumble. I fell to my knees again. I had to get to the car! I closed my eyes and muttered, "Please, Father, help me get to the car."

After I caught my breath, and still in the attitude of prayer, I heard a voice whisper, "Be still, and know that I am God; I will be exalted among the heathen, I will be exalted in the earth." I sat back on my heels and answered the voice, saying, "Here I am, God. I am willing to serve thee." I opened my eyes and saw Aaron sitting on a log in front of me. He smiled at me and said, "Are you feeling better now, Bishop?" "Yes," I said. "It is time. Make your way back to Walker."

I started crying and, through the tears, told him, "I don't have any paper." He reached over and put a gentle hand on my head and said, "Worry yourself no more. Because of your diligence in doing what you've been asked to do, I bless you with perfect clarity of mind. You will remember everything, word for word, until you write it down." With that, a light opened around him and I was alone again. As I got to my feet, I hurt everywhere. A smile crossed my lips and I spoke loudly, "You know, you could have given me a ride back."

I returned in the direction from which I had come. I struggled in the darkness for a while until a full moon crested the mountains and lit the valley below. I knelt down and thanked my Father in Heaven for the light he had sent. In the dim light I found I was a short distance from the hayfields at Spring Creek Ranch. At least now I could clearly see the trail. Although I still felt a great urgency to get back, I took time to get some water from a running stream nearby so I could drink and clean my cuts. This gave me renewed energy, and I started back for the mesa at a jogging pace.

As I reached the crest of the mesa, the clouds closed in on the moon. The fire had almost gone out; Walker usually kept it going until late in the evening. After I had rebuilt the fire, I walked over to the lean-to. As I cleared the door, the dancing flames illuminated the walls to show Walker's body lying on the floor; he was unconscious and his breathing was shallow. I looked down to see a pool of liquid reflecting the flickering light and realized that it was a pool of blood. Walker had severely broken his leg and the bone was protruding from the skin. I wondered what had happened while I was gone! The sight of his grotesquely torn leg made me sick to my stomach, and as I stood there watching the life being pumped out of him, I realized that my mind was numb and I was unable to act. I begged Heavenly Father to help me know what needed to be done, but if it was Walker's time to go, please let him go quickly. In an instant I had my answer; it was not yet Walker's time, and I knew exactly what to do to save his life. I yanked off my shirt and tore a sleeve off to make a tourniquet for the leg, which would stop the bleeding. I tried to reset the leg but couldn't get the bone to move! So I put my weight on the leg to straighten it out as much as possible. As I did this, I could see the bone moving back into the hole in Walker's leg. I eased up on the leg, releasing the pressure, and I could feel the bone sliding gently back into place. The tourniquet had stopped the bleeding for now, but I knew I had to take it off as soon as possible and cauterize the wound. I knew Walker had a pistol, so I looked around the lean-to and found it under his bedding. I flipped open the cylinder and dumped out the shells. Then I tore off a patch from my shirt, and because my adrenaline was so high, I was able to literally pop the lead from the shell casings, which made it possible for me to dump the powder from the shells onto the patch. When I had emptied all five shells, I left one in the cylinder out of respect for Walker's lifelong training to never have an empty pistol. I folded the patch and pushed it as deeply as I could into the wound. I then lit the gunpowder with a small twig from the fire. I gave it about two minutes and released the tourniquet; the bleeding was stopped. Walker moaned and twitched. After a few minutes more, he slowly opened his eyes.

"Bishop?" His voice was very thin, almost a whisper. "Is that you?"

"Yes, Walker. I'm here." "I'm still alive?"

"Yes, Walker. I didn't make it to my car because Aaron came and sent me back."

He tried to prop himself up but winced in pain and fell back to the floor. "How did I make it back up here?" he asked. I told him I didn't know, but from the looks of his hands and knees, it appeared that he had crawled. I had no idea how he had made it all the way back up to the top of the mesa. It must have taken a massive effort!

A few more moments passed before he opened his eyes again.

"I'm going to die." A thin smile crossed his emaciated and weathered face. "What happened?" I asked.

"I was . . . I . . . fell . . . my uncle . . . must ask forgiveness." His strength was fleeting, and I knew he didn't have long.

"Save your strength, my friend, I know there is more to your story. "Thanks," was the last word he spoke.

I sat there for a time in the flickering firelight watching the man who had become my friend. His breathing was steady but shallow. Sitting there, watching him breathe and not knowing which breath would be his last, caused a flood of memories of the events that started me on this journey to come into my mind.

My beloved wife, who was the best part of me, had died of cancer several years prior. Before we found out she had cancer, we had started reading the Pearl of Great Price, the Doctrine and Covenants, The Book of Mormon, and finally the Bible. This was quite an ambitious goal! All these books are considered scripture in our church. Throughout her life, my wife had spiritually prepared for the time when she would be called home. We had to suspend our reading while she was operated on and when she went through the first phase of chemotherapy. We were on our last book, the Bible, somewhere in Romans, when she went into a coma. I wanted to finish our goal before she died, so I read to her each day. One day, my wife's hospice nurse, whose name was Delores, asked me if she could read to her and I agreed to let her. I gave her the Bible already opened to the page I was reading, but for some reason she flipped to the beginning and started reading in Genesis. As Delores read, my wife started to thrash about. When Delores stopped reading, she seemed to settle down. When Delores started reading again, my wife started to thrash again. After several attempts, Delores called me in and told me what was going on. Because my wife was so familiar with the scriptures, she knew Delores was not reading where she should be. Delores went back to where I had left off and everything went smoothly after that. My wife died a few days after we finished the Bible.

I discovered something while my wife lay silently. Comatose people are still aware. Their mental faculties are sharpened, and they understand everything that is said around them. I believe that they are very close to God and that we should speak the truth in everything we say when we are around people in that condition. Because of my calling as a bishop in the church, I have had the great privilege of watching a number of people in the last stages of their lives. I know that reading the scriptures to someone who is dying helps them to have a peaceful end.

When my thoughts returned to the present, I realized Walker had slipped into a coma. I opened my scriptures and began reading aloud to Walker. I read to him for about half an hour and then paused to check on his status. His breathing continued to be raspy and labored. I knelt beside him and looked into his almost lifeless face. Though I had been forewarned of this event, I could not prevent myself from crying. Through the lump in my throat, I forced out the words "Walker, I have grown to truly love you, my brother."

It was at that moment I noticed a light gradually starting to build in the room. I looked up to see Aaron standing in the room looking at Walker, and I felt the great love he had for him. That was an experience which is beyond my ability to describe. He looked at me, smiled, and said, "I love him too." He moved to stand over me and placed his hand on my shoulder. "He has the greatest respect for you and would like you to take the last step of his journey with him." I bowed my head and fell to my knees. "Dear Lord, I am not worthy. Please make me clean."

"Bishop, please look behind you and see how far you have come." I did as I was told, and as I looked back, I was able to see all the struggles I'd had throughout my life. "You have worked all of your life at making yourself clean, so please tell me what you are concerned about."

"I can't bear the pain again of losing someone I love." I remembered my anguish as my beloved wife left this world. I turned back to look again into Walker's motionless face, and my chest felt as if it was being crushed. "Oh my God, my heart can't take this pain!"

"Bishop." The messenger's voice was soft, but it penetrated my soul. "The pain of which you speak is an illusion. Death is not the end. Come and witness Walker's rebirth in the next life." I bowed my head and thanked him as I felt warmth and comfort flowing through my entire body.

When I opened my eyes and stood up, I was no longer on the mesa. It's difficult to describe exactly where I was. It appeared that I was in an enormous room, but I'm certain I was outside because of the amount of vegetation and scenery around me. Everything was alive and vibrant. I had never seen a more perfect place!

There were a number of individuals gathered a distance from me welcoming someone home. After a short time, two men made their way toward me. I recognized Aaron, but the young man beside him wasn't familiar to me. He was a young Indian warrior striding with pride and power. I quickly realized that it was Walker—young, strong, and confident. He came up and embraced me. Tears filled his eyes and he said, "I love you too, my brother." He thanked me for being with him during this transition. Then he backed away and smiled. "I want to introduce you to someone." He let out a piercing whistle, and within seconds, Scotty came bounding toward me. He was not what I had expected. As a matter of fact he was quite unremarkable in appearance and obviously a mix of several different breeds. I asked Walker what breed was dominant in Scotty and he answered happily, "Mutt."

I apologized to him for running out of paper and not being there when he hurt himself. He slugged me in the shoulder. "You think that matters now? Look where we are!" He started dancing about, laughing and shouting as he bounded around. Aaron stood patiently beside us, allowing time for our reunion. I say time, but I'm not sure time passed at all. Aaron finally stepped forward and firmly stated, "Come. Let us begin our journey." He motioned ahead, but instead of us walking, our destination came to us. Apparently, in the next life one can travel by either walking or by thought. Your destination can come to you or you can go to it. It can be in the present, the past, or even in the future.

A scene opened before our eyes. It was a gigantic meeting of all of Heavenly Father's children where our future on earth was being decided. I noticed that there was one dynamic individual who spoke boldly and had a lot of followers. He was saying, "Let us make man like bricks and I will lead, guide, teach, and provide all things. I will have all those who follow me return to you and none will be lost." He called himself the Son of the Morning, but I recognized him as Lucifer, better known as Satan here on earth. My mind opened, and I understood why so many had followed him. He was a magnificent being—tall, good-looking, and an inspirational speaker. He closed his remarks by smiting his breast and saying, "I will ascend into Heaven and I will exalt my throne above the stars of God. I will sit on the mount of the congregation, and I will ascend above the heights of the clouds. I will be like the Most High."

Another stepped forward and said, "Let us make man like stones which are uncut by human hands and let the Holy Ghost be man's teacher who will guide him and help him find his way back home to You. All that has been created is Thine, so let the glory be Thine, forever." I recognized this man as Jehovah, Heavenly Father's firstborn son who also had many followers. On earth, this man is known as Jesus Christ, the Savior of all mankind.

Lucifer's plan was rejected by the righteous sons and daughters of God. Men cannot be controlled by force without rebellion; they would be suppressed and never reach their full potential. If you look closely at the character of each son and daughter of God, you will see freedom written in every heart. Under the universal natural law of freedom, Lucifer's plan was destined to fail.

Lucifer, and those unrighteous sons and daughters of God who followed him, were convinced their way was the only way. Consequently, they rejected our Savior's plan. One-third of the hosts of heaven were cast down to earth without bodies, never to gain one because they chose not to keep their first estate.

Aaron spoke, "Do you know the meaning of this?" I started to say I did, but the angel lifted his hand to let me know he was talking to Walker and I was only there to observe.

"I remember reading the fourteenth chapter of Isaiah, but I don't know the meaning of the brick and the stones," Walker replied.

Aaron stated that Lucifer, now Satan because of the rebellion, planned to make all mankind the same in intelligence, wealth, and material provision, kind of like bricks, each one being the same as the other. By doing so, he would command them in all things pertaining to the way they were to live. When you see bricks, they all look the same, and that is what Satan planned to do with the sons and daughters of God.

"Do you understand gravity and electricity?" Aaron asked Walker. Walker said, "I know what they are, but I don't know how they work."

"Gravity and electricity are bound by universal natural law. They will always act the same under the same conditions, no matter where you are in the universe. Order is maintained in the universe by and through these natural laws. To take each individual intellect and force it to react the same way places natural law at odds with itself. When forced to do anything, an individual will sooner or later rebel."

Aaron continued, "It takes mortar to hold bricks together. Lucifer's plan would have used material goods to control mankind like food, water, and warmth, which are all things man needs to survive. By controlling the necessities of life, he would then be able to control the sons and daughters of God and force them to do whatever he wanted them to do. However, not everyone would be equal. He would have to give power to kings, police, armies, and others to act as enforcers."

Aaron continued. "Stones, on the other hand, are created by God. Stones are large, small, hard, soft, and all different shapes. God commanded Adam to make an altar of stones untouched by hammer and chisel. By choosing wisely, Adam placed stones selectively and built an edifice that could not be destroyed. No mortar was needed because the natural contour of the stones locked tightly into place. Our Savior is the Divine Craftsman. He utilizes the unique abilities of each soul to build His kingdom. Take pebbles from the beach. They are all different, and when you put them in a rock tumbler and polish them, each one comes out beautiful in its own way. If we would all follow the Savior's plan, there would be no need for rulers, police, armies, or enforcers of any kind because we would all love one another."

Walker bowed his head and spoke softly, "He certainly had a challenge using me." Aaron continued, "They that rebelled with Satan did not go quietly."

My curiosity got the better of me and I had to ask, "What weapons do they use to continue their fight? They can't use physical tools because they are spirits."

"Look," said Aaron. "Those who were cast out were selecting weapons to fill their quivers. Arrows marked 'Lies' seemed to be their weapons of choice, but they also chose clubs, slings, and swords marked with words like 'Addiction,' 'Gold,' 'Silver,' 'Depression,' 'Loneliness,' 'Sexual Promiscuity,' 'Greed,' 'Gluttony,' 'Power,' 'Pride,' 'Enslavement,' 'Pornography,' and 'Divorce.'"

A puzzled look came over Walker. "The other weapons I can see clearly, but what is that one?" Before Aaron could respond, Walker answered his own question. "I understand now. It's marked 'Complacency.' They are using lukewarm attitudes like John spoke of in chapter 3 of Revelations where God said, 'They were neither hot nor cold and because they were lukewarm, He would spew them out of His mouth.'"

"You see well, Walker."

As we watched, Lucifer stepped forward and took only one weapon. I couldn't make out what it was. "Look closely," Aaron said.

"It looks like he has a little cord," I remarked.

"That is correct, Bishop. It is what we call a flaxen cord, and it is one of the reasons you are here. It is the most powerful weapon in his arsenal because it destroys freedom and it keeps many of Father's children from finding the truth. We will go back to your path, Walker, so you can see how strong and powerful that cord is. Look."

The view faded and changed back to the scene where Satan was being cast out. We could see the valiant ones who supported the Savior. They stepped forward, one by one, and were selected to experience life on earth. This fascinated me because they were sent to every corner of the world, and everywhere they went, the Savior's principles were taught. In most of the places, the Savior wasn't known and his teachings were never taught, but God sent the Holy Ghost (sometimes known as our conscious) to teach us good from bad. Also, He created the Spirit Prison where they could go and wait to be taught the gospel and decide rather to accept or reject it. (1 Peter 3:18-20)

My mind was set adrift in thought. I had always been told the Jews were the chosen people, but my brain would not accept the fact that Heavenly Father would send all these people to the earth and only give Israel the right to be the chosen ones. I thought of the wise men coming "from the East" to visit the Christ child. They already knew all about the Savior and had been waiting for his coming for who knows how long. Now that I had seen the Holy Ghost going to all parts of the earth, I understood how Christ's teachings, to one degree or another, are in every nation and every generation. God is no respecter of persons; all will have the opportunity to listen and to choose. All will be taught even if it is through messengers like Aaron who will instruct them as they pass to the next life.

Upon understanding this message, we were whisked away to the next great scene. We could see two great spirits coming to earth: a handsome baby boy to the Hopi nation and a beautiful baby girl to the Navajo nation. We were able to watch them grow up. They were both good children in every way. Both were tutored in all the ceremonial instruction of their respective nations, and both became knowledgeable and well-versed. Both were asked to lead their tribe in many dances, and both were asked to perform their rites and rituals on a national tour to educate others in the indigenous ways. It was at one of these performances that the two met.

It was love at first sight. There was purity in their love and a total respect for each other. If everyone conducted themselves the way these two did, most of the world's problems would be eliminated.

When the couple announced their engagement, both families were upset because each family had planned for their children to marry within their own tribe. "Can you see the cord?" Aaron asked. As the contention increased between the two families, we noticed that the flaxen cord was being wrapped and interwoven around each family pulling the families away from each other. The cord was very thin to the point of being almost invisible, but once someone was caught in it, it seemed impossible to break. The contention became so great the couple decided to leave both families and move to Albuquerque, New Mexico.

"Look," said Aaron, and we saw a messenger lead the spirit of a colt to a mare. The colt was born, and it was a beautiful Appaloosa with a black head and with an almost perfect white star between its eyes. Its coat was black a third of the way down its neck and then white the rest of the way almost to its hindquarters. The white area looked like a blanket laying on his neck and extending from his shoulders to his flank. His hindquarters were black with large white spots. The edges of the white spots were peppered with white and black hairs mixed together, which looked like shading around the spots. The breeders registered the colt, naming him Wahoo's Tail Star because the patterns on the colt looked like stars in the night sky.

The young man saw this beautiful colt in a pasture and instantly fell in love with it. His wife saw the passion her husband had for the animal and could not deny them from being together. So the two of them scrimped and saved every dime they had until they could buy the colt. The young man started Wahoo's training the moment they got him home. If he could have moved the horse into the house, he would have let the colt sleep on the bed with them. He spent long hours each day working with Wahoo, and the horse responded to whatever he was asked to do. The man's dear wife took great pleasure in watching her husband work with Wahoo. It wasn't long before Wahoo had won several big shows and people were bringing their mares to be bred to him. Wahoo's temperament was always well-mannered around man and beast, mirroring the temperament of his owner.

Then we saw a messenger lead the spirit of a child to the wife. Walker fell to his knees, and with tears flowing, he turned to me and said, "They are my father and mother."

The angel put his hand on Walker's head and told him he was correct. "Their names are Tadi, which means 'Wind,' and Nita, which means 'Strong.'"

During our days together, Walker had mentioned that his uncle taught him that his dad was a great hunter. I could now see that his dad was a professional hunting guide who was successful enough to have three to six men working for him at any one time. They took hunters from all over the world on pack trips, and they hunted anything one can get a license to hunt. They even took people to hunt rabbits and prairie dogs.

We saw Walker there. He must have been around the age of two because he was walking. The guides were preparing for another hunting trip, and by the amount of supplies they had, it appeared that a large group would be trekking out. Surprisingly, there were only three hunters going! There was an incredible amount of excess goods because the hunters wanted to be comfortable. It was funny watching Walker always underfoot. No one cared. They just picked him up and moved him out of the way. As soon as they set him down, he was into something else.

Nita didn't like the three men because they treated her husband more like a slave than a guide. It's funny what money will do to some people. As they made ready to leave, Nita did something she had never done before. She stopped her husband and told him she had a bad feeling and asked him not to go. Tadi sat on the doorstep for a few minutes and then told her, "I can't stand to refuse you anything, my love. Please never ask anything of me which you know I will have to refuse." She paused for a moment, pondering whether or not she should tell him of the child she bore. She decided it was best to wait until his return when they could celebrate the coming of their new addition together.

As we witnessed the scenes and circumstances of Walker's life, it was unlike anything I had witnessed before. I had watched movies and television, but now there was an interaction with each scene that put us into the story. As different events unfolded, heavenly messengers would speak to each individual, helping to guide them in their actions. The messengers were not seen by those they guided, but we witnessed them moving toward and away from each person. At times they would whisper, and their suggestions would be followed. More often they were completely ignored, causing them to be as loud and as forceful as they could possibly be to get the attention of their wards. As we watched Tadi say goodbye to Nita, one messenger was telling Tadi not to leave. Another messenger was pleading with Nita to tell him of the treasure she held inside. Both were ignored.

The hunters packed into the wilderness traveling for ten hours before stopping and setting up camp. They didn't appear to be "roughing it" as their camp was lavishly set up. One could barely even call it camping! Each of the hunters brought what looked like a double bed, and each of their huge tents was set up with a heater. There was a separate tent for the kitchen and their chef. As if to enforce the elitist theme of the camp, the guides chose to sleep in the open under the stars.

They were up and going before daylight. Tadi carried only a bow and arrows, using them with skill and accuracy when the clients failed to kill the animals with their rifles. Most of the time, all the hunters wanted from their prey were the antlers. They allowed the guides to take the meat home to their families.

Tadi was meticulous in how he set up the hunt. The demands of the hunters before entering the wild were tempered by the knowledge and skill of Tadi and his men, and soon they were following his orders without question. The first day's hunt began before sunrise. At the edge of a small clearing, Tadi began to call the elk, insisting the hunters remain quiet in the trees behind him. Nothing stirred all morning, so the hunters moved out of the trees onto a grassy knoll, letting the sun warm them while they took a long nap. They were not allowed to smoke, drink, or build a fire because Tadi did not want any unnecessary odors scaring the game. After the nap, the hunters were ready for a chance to find their prey.

Evening came, and as the air cooled, Tadi started calling again. A large bull entered the clearing, but before they could shoot, another large bull crashed through the brush. The two six-point bulls were shot within twenty-five feet of each other. The hunters partied into the night praising themselves for their conquests. The guides did their best to quiet the three, but as the alcohol was poured, the noise increased. The next day the game was scarce. They saw two cows but no bulls. By the third day it was obvious they would have to break camp and find another location to fill the third and final tag. But, because it was so warm, it was decided that they would have to get the meat they already had out before it spoiled. Despite knowing of Nita's misgivings, Tadi wanted the selection of the person taking out the meat to be fair. They decided to draw straws, and as luck would have it, Tadi drew the short straw. Carrying out the meat, the trash, and a few trivialities the hunters felt they could do without, required six pack horses.

About an hour into the trek, Tadi was faced with the choice between two trails. One was six hours longer and was a fairly good trail, though somewhat rough. The other trail was much shorter, but it had four difficult and dangerous areas over which he would have to pass. One of Tadi's messengers encouraged him to take the long way. He pondered the decision for a few minutes and almost took the long trail but finally decided on the shorter one. The messenger screamed for him to change his mind and then watched as the pack moved down the trail.

In the first half hour, he traversed two of the rough passes that would have been bad enough with one horse, let alone six loaded down with elk and extras. This should have provided Tadi with enough warning to turn back, but still he pushed on. The trail, which was only wide enough for the horses to walk in single file, took a steep descent along the canyon wall, which was about three hundred feet above the canyon floor. It was more of a small game trail than a legitimate pack trail. A short way down, the trail changed from solid sandstone to shale, which was slick and unstable. Tadi dismounted to check the trail for signs of game; there weren't any. He knew that game not using a trail is an indication it might not be passable. Again, we witnessed a messenger encouraging him to turn back. He paused for a moment, as if listening, but then started to mount. The messenger forcefully told him to walk the horses, and after pausing again, he decided to lead the train on foot. As they entered the shale, Wahoo nervously pulled back, perhaps sensing the danger of the steep drop-off from the canyon wall and the instability of the slick layers of rock underfoot. Tadi spoke gently to calm the horse while leading the animals down the precarious cliffside trail. Again, the messenger warned Tadi not to continue down the trail. Tadi turned to face the horses, as if thinking about turning back, but realized it was too late. It would be almost impossible to get the horses back up the trail because there was no way to turn them around.

As they proceeded, Tadi found the footing much worse than he had anticipated; rain from the previous week had loosened the rock considerably. Suddenly, the sandstone rim, about thirty feet above them now, released a fairly large chunk of shale. It struck the third horse in the train, spooking him and knocking him off the trail, which sent him over the edge and down the sloping side of the canyon. Luckily, the lead rope on the horse behind him came loose which saved the last three horses from the fall. However, the tie on the horse in front of the falling horse, and on Wahoo, held fast, so both horses went over the edge with the horse that had fallen. Tadi saw the terror in Wahoo's eyes as he slid toward the edge. Instead of letting go of the reins and releasing the horse to its doom, Tadi dug his heels in and tried to stop the fall, but he was quickly pulled over the edge too. In slow motion, we saw the three horses and Tadi tumbling head over heels down the rocky terrain as they made their way to the bottom of the canyon. We saw arrows from Tadi's quiver flying from their sheath and becoming lodged in the shale, some with their points turned upward. As Wahoo continued his tumbling descent, we saw him roll onto an arrow, which punctured a lung and penetrated his heart. The magnificent animal was dead before he landed. The horse behind Wahoo broke its back when it landed on top of the first horse that had gone over the edge and both horses were badly cut and making pitiful, gut-wrenching sounds. Tadi was partly under Wahoo when the movement stopped. During the fall, one of the razor-sharp arrows freed from Tadi's quiver sliced through the back part of Tadi's leg a little above the knee, severing an artery.

Since he couldn't get out from under his horse, he bled to death next to the friend he had loved so much.

As Tadi's spirit left his body, we saw the messenger standing next to him. He greeted Tadi warmly with a gesture, as if to say, "What else could I have done?"

Tadi's first question was, "What about my son?"

"You mean sons. They will both find their own way. They both have a mission." "My wife will never forgive me. What will she do?"

"All will be made known to you in the proper time. She has a fight ahead of her, and she will have another baby boy." The messenger placed his hand on Tadi's shoulder. "Come." As each one mounted a horse, a light opened around them and in an instant they were gone.

The remaining horses worked their way back up the trail until they could turn around. They slowly returned to camp, and it was evening before they were spotted standing next to the other horses. The entire camp scrambled to search. The six horses of Tadi's train made quite a trail, so the guides were able to track them after dark. They found where the horses had gone over the steep bank, and all the men made their way down the treacherous shale slide to Tadi and the horses. The scene was a gruesome one. The horse with the broken back had died sometime during the day, and they found the last horse all but dead from the deep gashes on its legs and side. They had to put the horse down. Lastly, they found Tadi's dead body laying underneath his beloved Wahoo. Like a well-oiled team, they all worked together silently in the dark retrieving Tadi. The guides decided it would be best to get back to town and take the camp down later. The three hunters said there was nothing in the camp they wanted, so they headed for home.

Nita was in a daze, numb from the thought of life without her love. It was apparent to us that she would never recover from her loss and that her life on earth was as good as over. The two families argued where Nita and Walker should live. I noticed, again, the cord surrounding Nita's family. They argued that she was Navajo, not Hopi, and that she, being pregnant, needed her family. All the time you could see those cords pulling tighter and getting stronger. Her family finally prevailed and took her home. For months she fought to make sense of her loss, and she hated how her parents treated Walker. Nita finally found the courage to stand up to her parents, screaming at them and walking out. A couple of weeks later her mom and dad were killed in a head-on collision just outside of Santa Fe, New Mexico. I looked over to see tears well up in Walker's eyes as he watched the anguish his mother had gone through.

Six months passed. A registered letter finally found Nita who was now living in a trailer near her parent's property. Inside was a signed blank check. The letter stated that the three hunters had set up a trust fund for Walker and Nita with part of the funds being put into an education account and the other part in a life annuity. The instructions were simple: buy a home wherever you want to live and pay for it with this check. There were three business cards and an additional letter with instructions for an attorney on how to proceed. It was up to Nita to go to an attorney of her choice for assistance with all the transactions. She took Walker over to the neighbor's and asked the girl if she would take care of him for a couple of hours. With no car, Nita started walking the four miles to town. Her joy made the distance seem like a walk around the block. Halfway to town, a pickup going in the opposite direction pulled up close to her and two men jumped out and grabbed her. She fought with all her might and almost got away. A third man, the driver of the truck, stepped in and hit her in the back of the head with his fist and knocked her out. They taped her hands and feet together with black electrician's tape and gagged her. Then they put her into the back of the pickup and covered her with a tarp.

Aaron turned to Walker. "This will not be pleasant. You have a choice. We can witness all the details or I can tell you what happened to your mother."

"I need to see," said Walker.

"Very well." The scene continued. A messenger was under the tarp with Nita. He told her to be calm and patient because she was not going to be able to get away. He instructed her to destroy the check. She worked it out of her pocket and was able to tear it twice before allowing the wind to sweep it out of the pickup. The messenger whispered to her that her babies would be well cared for. He continued, "A couple will come to you asking you to sign papers to adopt your unborn baby. Please sign the papers."

Walker, Aaron, and I watched as she was beaten and abused. She fought whenever she could, pulling out handsful of her attackers' hair, scratching and biting and drawing blood whenever she could; she was determined not to submit to them. Nita's attackers decided that the only way she could be controlled was with drugs. We watched as she was slowly destroyed by the drugs and the abuse. Walker, with tears streaming down his face, placed his hand on Aaron's shoulder. "Please stop. I can't take any more."

The angel brought the scene to a close saying, "She fought every inch of the way. You were never out of her conscious thoughts, and she did everything she could to protect her unborn baby. The drugs forced her into labor and she had the baby six weeks early."

"Walker, look." Walker could now see Buddy entering the room where Nita had been taken. One of the men in the room stopped him briefly but then listened to a messenger telling him to let Buddy go without causing any trouble. The men knew they were in trouble and were scrambling to get out before the police came. The man who confronted Buddy accidently dropped a letter with his name and address on it, so the police were able to find him. When they did, he refused to tell them where Nita had been taken. Because she could not be controlled, the "cartel," as they called themselves, decided to get rid of Nita. Interestingly, the man who confronted Buddy in the motel room had fallen in love with Nita, so he hid her from them. While she was in hiding, the drugs wore off. Nita asked the man to untie her, and when he did, she sprang like a wildcat, grabbing him by the head and trying to bite through the vein in his neck. Because she was so weak, she only succeeded in biting off his ear lobe. By sheer strength and weight, the man was able to subdue her again.

Buddy hired two detectives to find the people who had Nita. They were only able to find the man who was hiding her. Their interrogation tactics were far different from those the police used, and Nita was soon rescued and immediately taken to the hospital. The detectives brought Kathy and Buddy to the hospital, and when they asked Nita to sign the adoption papers, she did. She asked Kathy and Buddy to please find her four-year-old son and take care of him too. "This is when the search for you started, Walker," said Aaron. "When they found you, the only way they could get you into their care was through the LDS Placement Program. Initially, they were only going to keep you until your mother got out of rehab. They already had Robbie, and the Holy Ghost confirmed that it would be right for them to adopt him, which they did. The reason they never told you Robbie was your brother was because they weren't sure they would be able to adopt you. And it would have made it much more difficult for you when you were placed back onto the reservation with your aunt and uncle."

I looked at Walker and saw that he had tears in his eyes. "I always knew Robbie was my brother," he whispered.

"Look," said the angel. The man who left the letter turned state's evidence on the other guys. This broke up a sex-slave ring involving nine other people. We watched as they were brought before the judge. Three of them were totally bound by the flaxen cords. They were second-generation sex slaves, since their fathers had been in the business before them. This was where Aaron instructed us on how Satan uses the traditions of the fathers to control generation upon generation with sin, hate, and lies being passed down from fathers to sons.

The man went to court and pled guilty, but he still received life in prison. Hearing the voice of the messenger in the motel room changed him. He spent his time working with gang members trying to help free them from their gang affiliations. He was very effective and made many enemies. Consequently, he was stabbed in the back and killed by another inmate with a homemade knife.

"Look again." Nita was going through hell, not so much in detox, but from trying to overcome the mental defenses she had developed while in captivity. She spent over a year getting clean, and when she left the halfway house, she started looking for Buddy and Kathy. She no longer had their address, and because of the adoption, Robbie's papers were sealed. Buddy, however, had been monitoring Nita's progress and had made contact with her soon after she found a trailer of her own. He made arrangements for her to come and see her boys. Buddy had purchased bus tickets and had instructed her to pick them up, but as she was crossing the street near the ticket office, two young boys high on drugs hit her with their car. Thinking she was dead, they put her in the trunk and took her way out into the desert.

"Look." Tadi was in the trunk of the car with her, and he was telling her to stop fighting it; it was time for her to come home. She wouldn't stop fighting death until she was promised Kathy and Buddy would always do what was best for the boys. Tadi assured her that they would be well cared for, and as she released her grip on this world, he lifted her into his arms and kissed her.

Aaron gripped Walker by the shoulder. "There is someone here waiting to meet you." They turned about to see Tadi and Nita waiting patiently to greet him.

"Son." Walker fell into their embrace, weeping openly. They held each other tightly for a long while before he could compose himself.

"I'm so sorry," said Walker. "For what, son?"

"For what I thought of you all my life."

"This is a place of forgiveness. If you open your heart, all is revealed. It's now up to you to forgive yourself. Your Heavenly Father has already forgiven you."

After a long reunion, Aaron interrupted. "Tadi, Nita, excuse us please. Walker is not finished with his orientation."

As Walker's mother and father embraced him once again, they turned to me and said, "Thank you for being with our son during his most difficult trial. You were the answer to our prayers."

Once again, Aaron said, "Look." We looked and saw that the two boys who had hit Nita had parked their car among some old, abandoned cars on the reservation. They got out and walked quite a way from the car to discuss what to do. Both boys decided to go back and turn themselves in.

"Aaron, why are you showing me the story of those two? I know what happened to my mother and I don't care to see what happens to those two guys!"

"Remember, if your heart is open, all will be revealed. There is a lesson here that is important for the bishop to write. Look."

The two boys started back for the car but got turned around and walked in the wrong direction. They had traveled a long way, and as the drugs wore off, they discovered themselves in the wilderness, lost. They panicked, and instead of retracing their steps, they started running, all the time getting farther from the car and deeper into the desert. Four days and nights passed, and they had covered an amazing distance, passing from Arizona into Colorado. The older boy succumbed to thirst and the elements. The younger boy was trying to bury him when a messenger spoke to him telling him to leave his brother and go over the hill. He obeyed and found a Navajo sheepherder on the other side of the hill. The sheepherder gave the boy some water but could not understand him. The herder left his flock and took him to Shiprock, and from there he was transferred to a hospital in Cortez. It took him almost a week to recover enough to tell the authorities what had happened. A search was made and the older brother was found.

A massive search was made for the car, but it couldn't be located. Since the boy was originally from California and unfamiliar with that area, he wasn't able to tell them where the girl and the car were. Because of that, the doctors came to the conclusion that the accident was a delusion.

The boy tried to convey to everyone what he had done. With no evidence, and with the doctor's conclusion, no one believed him. His frustration became so great that he reached the point of taking his own life. As he prepared to do so, two LDS missionaries knocked on his door. He accepted the Gospel of Jesus Christ as if he had known it all his life.

The boy related his story to a young missionary leader who was helping him prepare for his baptism. The interviewer decided that it would take a higher authority to decide if he could be forgiven for the crimes he committed and postponed the baptism. The story was related to the mission president, and after much prayer and fasting, he finally received the answer that the young man had done all he could to make things right. He would be able to call upon the Savior's atonement. This process made him doubt his worthiness. We watched as he put off his baptism, time and again, unable to forgive himself. It was like he was trying to punish himself for his sins. One night, as he sat alone in total despair, the Savior appeared to him in a dream. He told him to have faith in His sacrifice and Atonement. He took the young man with Him into the Garden where His suffering for all the sins of mankind was so great He bled from every pore in His body. Then the Savior took him all the way through His trial and crucifixion. He told the young man He had paid this horrible price and had the power and authority to forgive his sins. He said, "I have forgiven you, and now in order to be healed, you must forgive yourself." The Savior told the young man he wanted him to sing the praises of the Atonement and of His forgiveness. This puzzled the young man because he knew he couldn't carry a tune in a bucket. Nevertheless, he was baptized the next day. As he came up out of the water, we saw that the cords had fallen from him and that he was completely cleansed. "Take this message to the world, Bishop. When you forgive yourself and others, you become whole."

The young man started a new life. He met a successful businessman who used to be a local leader, or Stake President, over several wards, i.e., congregations for The Church of Jesus Christ of Latter- day Saints and related his story. The two of them started a survival camp for abused and troubled youth. He counseled people on how they had to forgive the abusers before the healing could come into their own lives, but that didn't mean to allow the abuse to continue. Every effort was made to remove these children from the abuse. They based their whole program on what the missionaries taught him out of the Doctrine of Covenants (Considered scripture by the Church of Jesus Christ of Latter Day Saints). Doctrine of Covenants 64:10 I, the Lord, will ᵃforgive whom I will forgive, but of you it is required to ᵇforgive all men. 11 And ye ought to say in your hearts – let God a judge between me and thee, and reward thee according to the ᶜdeeds. This is so powerful because if you are living fear or hate that person has control over your mind and can torture you every day. But if you forgive and let God take care of them you can become free and put our life back together. Honestly, this is the most healing doctrine I have ever known. Now I see the point the angel was making.

Every day when a child wakes up and his mind dwells on the abuse, the abuser continues to have power over him. The children continue to be mentally abused every day, even when removed from the situation. Unless they can forgive they will not be able to move on. As I looked at the children, I could see the cords wrapped around them and their families, choking out generation after generation.

As these young people came to an understanding of forgiveness, the cords lost their grip and fell to the ground. They stepped beyond the cords, leaving them behind. The healing was so complete that most of the youth dedicated their lives to helping others who had the same problem. We saw Satan's outrage at their success. He dedicated his full forces to stopping the program, but the program was dedicated to God, so Satan couldn't defeat it. In his own way, the young man sang the praises of the Savior's atonement and forgiveness all the rest of his life.

Aaron said look. We saw Nita and this young man and the man from the motel come into the presence of the Lord. Before they came to Earth they were best of friends. Both men were weak and afraid they wouldn't make it back. Nita, having much more faith and spiritual strength, petitioned Heavenly Father before her journey to earth to find a way to bring them home together. She promised to do anything necessary to help them return. Her sacrifice allowed each man to repent, and after doing so, each one helped many other people to find their way home. 'When ye have done this to the least of these thy brethren, ye have done it unto me.' 'If, in this life only, we have hope in Christ, we are of all men most miserable.' Ponder these words, Walker, and I shall return shortly."

Walker and I then found ourselves sitting on the edge of a mesa watching the sun kiss the valley. We sat there for a long time without saying anything before Walker turned to me and said, "We are in the Spirit Prison." The beauty of this place was amazing, but I knew he was right. It's no wonder people mistakenly called this place "Heaven."

As the valley filled with light, I sat musing. "If this is the Spirit Prison, I wonder what Paradise is like!"

CHAPTER 15

MY BOOK OF LIFE IS REVEALED

"**B**ishop, why are we here? I've always believed the Spirit Prison was a place of instruction to help us prepare to enter into Paradise. What I don't understand is why we're here right now. Maybe my baptism wasn't properly done."

"Walker, I know that your baptism was properly done, but I also know that you have a lot of questions that haven't been answered yet, and this is the place where you will get all the answers." We sat for a while, pondering, as we watched the colors dance through the valley, manipulated by sun and shadows.

Walker was first to break the silence. "I remember a family home evening where we talked about the Spirit Prison." He paused for a moment and grinned. "This is amazing! I can totally recall every detail of that night, including the tastes and smells!" The grin broke into a broad smile. "Mom prepared a wonderful dessert of baked apples with cinnamon and raisins. It was her turn to teach the lesson, and she chose a scripture to talk about. The scripture was 1 Peter 3:18–20. 'For Christ also had once suffered for sins, the just for the unjust, that he might bring us to God, being put to death in the flesh, quickened by the Spirit: By which also he went and preached unto the spirits in prison: Which sometime were disobedient, when once the longsuffering of God waited in the days of Noah, while the ark was a preparing, wherein few, that is, eight souls were saved by water.' Just like baptism saves us. I remember every detail in the same way as we viewed the deaths of my birth father and mother." As he sat on the cliff beside me, I noticed that he was joyful as he recalled everything about that evening.

I let him enjoy the moment while I pondered why I was here. The amount of information I was now privileged to know scared me. Why would Father want me to witness all this? Does this mean that my time is at hand as well? Will I even have the opportunity to finish writing Walker's story? Then it hit me. I know why Walker came here to the Spirit Prison. "Walker, you're not here to stay."

"What do you mean?"

"Father brought us here to our cliff on the mesa to allow you to recognize how learning takes place here in the Spirit Prison. You won't always have a guide or instructors to cater to your every whim. You're experiencing an orientation to help you realize what you want to know and how to continue to learn. Sitting by yourself is merely a means to open your memory. The instruction is to fill in the gaps."

Walker sat briefly then stood up and beckoned me to join him. "You speak the truth. It's time to continue our journey to Paradise."

"That is right, Walker." Aaron was standing with us, and he placed his hand on Walker's shoulder. "Come." He pointed to the scene in Walker's home when the people from the agency were there to pick him up. It was one thing to have Walker tell the story, but to actually see it added a dimension I didn't expect. Buddy scared the daylights out of me when he jumped up and went screaming into the bedroom to grab his rifle. And to watch him fall to his knees begging God to stop them from taking his son was truly heart wrenching. I found that I could actually feel what he was feeling.

"Look." Walker was in the car with the three social workers and before Walker were two paths. One was narrow and straight, and the other veered off to the left and was rough and crooked. Walker chose the crooked path when he decided to reach across and threaten the two people in the front seat. As Walker took the crooked path, something interesting happened. A heavenly messenger whispered to Robbie, "It's up to you to take Walker's place and help lead this family." He listened and started down the straight path.

Walker began to cry. "Robbie was always my support and example. He always seemed to be there to clean up any messes I made, and he was always willing to fill in with my chores when I wanted to do something else. I don't think I ever really appreciated him."

"Look." We saw that Robbie was now old enough to go on a mission for the church, but his health was so bad his bishop was very concerned about his leaving home for the required two years. Buddy and Kathy wrote a letter to the general authorities of the church asking them for their permission for Robbie to go, and for a special blessing for him so that he would be able to fulfill a mission for the church. They soon received a letter back saying that Robbie was to go on a mission and that he would be strengthened and protected. We continued watching and saw Robbie dragging himself around on crutches from door to door. The MS had made him almost completely immobile, but we could see that his spirit would not quit; he went everywhere with a smile and enthusiasm. As missionaries go out in pairs, there were times when his companion wanted to pick him up and carry him back to their home. Each of Robbie's companions throughout his mission gained too much respect for him to even ask if they could help. The next morning Robbie was up and at it again.

They were serving in Mexico, and as they worked with numerous families, we could see that these families were heavily woven with Satan's flaxen cords. Time after time, wonderful people told the missionaries their parents and grandparents had believed this way all their lives and it would be too hard to change. Those traditions of the parents and grandparents only strengthened the cords around them and kept them from accepting the gospel.

Robbie's determination was unconquerable. He was close to the Lord and the Lord's Spirit was with him. Like a sword, it sliced through the cords that bound families to their false traditions. Consequently, many did accept the gospel and join the church. We were able to see the cords falling away as they stepped from the waters of baptism. Each individual Robbie influenced made Satan throw a tirade. It seemed actually comical to be watching this from our vantage point. All of Satan's fussing and fighting made little impact. He really doesn't have much power when people decide to cast him from their lives.

Robbie had to put every ounce of himself into his mission, and with God's help, he completed his two years. Many of the Mexican people were very sad when he left their country. Robbie returned home to a hero's welcome, and the heavens broke open with great rejoicing.

Aaron stopped the images before us and turned to Walker. "You had as much to do with Robbie's success as he did. Your influence throughout his life helped him develop the determination which drove him through his mission, and your sacrifice inspired him. The Father would like you to prepare to greet him and be with him when he returns home."

"But I am unworthy of such a privilege," Walker responded.

Aaron put his arm around Walker and pointed to his heart. "Worthiness begins here. You will be worthy. Look."

The image opened again and Robbie was back in school. Before he started his last year of college he made a trip to Mexico and brought back one of the girls he had baptized during his mission. Lucinda was strong in the church and pure of heart and mind. She was like an angel. They were married the year before Robbie graduated, and his graduation celebration was cut short by the birth of his first son. A little over a year later they had twin boys. His health continued to decline, but they wanted one more child to complete their family. Two years after the twins were born, a little girl was added. They named her Nita.

Boys are wonderful, but when a beautiful little baby girl is placed in a father's arms, his heart melts and he becomes a different person. This is the way it was with Robbie. I have never seen such devotion as Robbie and Lucinda had to one another and to their children.

When the men who had gone hunting with Tadi saw that the check they had given to Nita hadn't been cashed, they searched for a relative and found Jimmie Begay. He told them of Robbie's illness, and they immediately reissued the check so Robbie and Lucinda could buy a home. The hunters also established an annuity for Lucinda and the children so they would be taken care of for the rest of their lives after Robbie died. Knowing that his family would be secure without him, Robbie was ready to be released from this life. He passed away a short time later. Because of the type of person Robbie was, I thought there would be a lot of mourning by his wife and family, but there wasn't. Lucinda was prepared, and knowing that she and Robbie would be together again for all time and eternity was a great comfort to her.

We then saw Walker greeting Robbie. We watched as the two embraced for a long time before Walker ushered Robbie straight into the presence of the Savior. The heavens rejoiced at his return.

"This hasn't happened yet!" Walker spoke up as he watched himself greet Robbie.

"Time has no bearing here." Aaron smiled as he answered. "You each have made the decisions which have led you to this conclusion. Here, it is already done."

"So I can find out what has happened on earth long before it ever happens?"

Aaron laughed. This gave me pause because it was the first time I'd heard him laugh; an angel's laugh is quite lyrical. "It is a simplified version of what is, but yes, Walker, we can witness things before they happen on earth."

The mood changed quickly, and Walker, with a contrite voice, asked, "What happened to the woman and the man from the agency, the two I threatened . . . when I took the crooked path?"

"Look." Walker was taking the wallet from the fat lady who had taken him from his home. Watching her now, I realized Walker's description of her as "the fat lady" was from the perspective of adolescence. Even though she was overweight, the best way to describe her was "the empty lady." It was apparent through her actions and her words that there was something missing in her life.

Walker took her license and put it into his pocket. She didn't actually work for the agency but was working for a group protesting the LDS Indian Placement Program. The incident with Walker left her so terrified that she quit her job and moved. She became so fearful that she even bought a gun and slept with it under her pillow.

"Look." We could see a man with a drinking problem. He was very cruel to his children and especially cruel to the oldest boy, the empty woman's father. When the boy married and had a child of his own, he became extremely jealous of the child and he carried on his father's tradition of abuse. He took it out on his daughter, the young empty woman. The same cords that bound the father were now binding his son, and the son was now passing the abuse on to his daughter.

We were horrified by what was happening and asked Aaron to take the image from us, but instead, he expanded the image to include every messenger who had supported that sweet young girl as she dealt with the unspeakable acts we witnessed. Fortunately, Aaron did narrow the view, so we were not privy to the months and years she endured the torture at home. She became pregnant, but after one severe beating we watched as the child was taken from her and escorted straight into the arms of the Savior.

The young empty woman was bleeding so badly she had to be taken to a hospital. Again, concourses of angels worked tirelessly with the staff of attentive nurses to help her in this dire situation. When she recovered, she was placed into a foster home where she started using food for comfort. Ultimately, by using food to try to assuage her misery, she gained a large amount of weight. She took the job with the protest group and found power that allowed her to take her misery out on other people.

"Look." We looked and saw that the empty lady had suffered a complete nervous breakdown from the paranoia Walker had instilled in her. She finally listened to her messenger and checked into an institution. For the first time in her life she was able to talk about the torture that had caused her so much misery and pain. As she did this, the turmoil inside of her quieted and her outside appearance changed. She no longer needed food for comfort, so the excess pounds fell off, and we saw a beautiful young woman emerge.

Searching for meaning to her existence, she discovered a natural talent for playing the piano. The music filled the void, and she practiced endlessly, finding pleasure and peace in the melodies. Shortly after she was released, she sought out an instructor. He was a religious and faithful man whose whole life was connected to God through music. It was through him she found Jesus, and the two became complete in each other.

We watched as she and the music teacher were married, and we saw her pray every night for Walker's forgiveness. As we stood watching, Walker left our side and walked up to her as she was kneeling in prayer. He put his arm around her and whispered, "I forgive you. Please forgive me." Even though she didn't know Walker was there, they were both brought to tears as they knelt together. I couldn't believe that this was happening right before my eyes! Walker got up and returned to stand next to Aaron and me.

The images of her life continued, and we saw three of the most beautiful daughters I believe I have ever seen. She treated her children and her husband with gentleness and respect. I somehow hadn't noticed before, but as I watched her interact with her children, I saw that the cords that had choked her for so long were completely gone. She was clean, as were her children. The traditions of her husband hadn't caused the children to be bound. Instead of being bound by Satan's flaxen cords, they were bound together by music and love. His family came from a long line of great musicians, and the light of the music had driven away the darkness. Satan fumed in complete disgust and defeat. She no longer fit the description of either "the fat lady" or "the empty lady."

Aaron spoke up as he read my thoughts. "Her name is Tracy Evans. Look."

An old man was before us, so bound with the cords it was hard to tell that he was even a man, and he was living in the worst filth anyone could imagine. This man was totally destroyed, passed out drunk and sitting in a tattered armchair. The door opened, and Tracy and her husband walked into the room. The old man was her father, Thomas Collins. Tracy's husband picked Thomas up and helped him to the car. They took him home and worked on sobering him up. As he started coming to his senses, he screamed horrible obscenities at them. Tracy left the room to escape the evil she felt there. As Tracy's husband, Todd, continued the process of dealing with the man, we heard a piano begin to play in the background.

After Thomas was cleaned up, they took him to an institution offering alcohol and drug rehabilitation. Thomas was totally irate, kicking and screaming at the prospect of being left in that place. As quickly as possible, he was sedated and taken to his room.

Two Saturdays each month Tracy and Todd went to the facility and put on a ragtime show for the people receiving treatment. It was a professional and fabulous affair. Tracy and Todd dueled on the piano for over an hour, shifting between songs, faster and faster until they were both playing different songs on the same piano at the same time. It ended when the two songs melded into one.

Tracy and Todd's three girls, now grown, had a comedy routine that almost put people into the hospital from laughter. They performed in three different states at different venues, but when they came home, they always found time to perform with their mom and dad. Their act of music and comedy was one of the greatest shows I'd ever witnessed, not because of the professionalism, but because of the love the family members shared, which was almost tangible.

After the performances, they spent one-on-one time talking to those going through treatment.

For some, this family was the only thing they had to hold on to.

The Evans had a good income, yet they lived modestly. Shortly after they were married, they sat down and established all their wants and needs. They also decided what causes they would contribute to. At first they could only contribute time, but as they became more financially stable, money was also included with their time. They had a solid savings program and no debt. All their expendable income was donated to their special causes and charitable organizations. They had a very positive influence on a large number of lives that were on the edge of destruction.

"Do you understand what you have seen?"

I went to answer, and again, Aaron stopped me and motioned to Walker.

"Not all traditions bring bondage. When properly chosen through thought and prayer, the right kinds bring freedom."

"Look." Thomas was living in an upstairs room in the Evans home. As Tracy practiced the piano, he would sit at the top of the stairs and let his troubled mind drift off with the music. The innocence of the music made him feel like a child. Tracy was aware of his presence but didn't ask him to join her at first. She knew how the music had healed her, so she allowed it to work on him before asking him to come down. If she stopped to invite him, he would scamper off to his room like a little child who was supposed to be in bed but was caught watching his parents at a party.

Tracy's piano was on a raised platform in a bay window, which was a beautiful setting for it. She knew the perfect way to include her father in her practice sessions. She purchased a huge recliner and had it delivered to her home. Once removed from its packaging, she dragged it over to the platform. Trying with all her might, she could not get it up the two steps. She reached the point of exhaustion and sat on the edge, staring at it, praying to know what to do. We watched a messenger whisper to her to tip the recliner over so the top part of the recliner was lying on the platform, and lift up the back end and scoot it until it was completely on. She did as she was instructed without hesitation, which was an incredible difference from what the fat lady would have done. She smiled, admiring her beautiful piano in the fabulous window setting with the recliner, which was totally out of place.

Tracy went up to her father's room, took him by the hand, and led him to his new throne. Tears welled in his eyes as he sat down and she began to play. Every day he would sit there and let his mind find peace while she played.

One day he got up and kneeled at her feet while she played and told her how proud he was of who she had become. He bowed his head and asked her if she could ever forgive him for what he had done to her. She took him by the arm and helped him to the piano bench beside her. She told him of the young boy she had torn from the only real home he had ever known because of the anger in her heart. In retaliation, this young man had taken a powerless situation and threatened her so completely that it shook her to the core. It was then that she realized she was more afraid of what she had become than she was of the threat of the young man. This prompted her to start seeing a psychologist who helped her to be able to forgive her father for the evil he had done. It was after she had forgiven him that she began to find peace.

She said, "Thomas . . . Dad, for years I was tortured by the thought of the evil I had done to that boy, and I prayed to God every day for mercy. One night as I prayed, this boy came to me and he forgave me. I knew, then, that God had truly forgiven me. Dad, you have taken many of the same steps to change your life. For many years I found it unthinkable to forgive you. Now, as I look at you, I know you deserve forgiveness."

He put his head in her lap, and his tears ran like a river onto the skirt of her dress.

Tracy's father had always gone to church with the family, but time after time, he stood at the door unable to go in. This poor man couldn't believe the Savior would truly forgive him because of what he had done. We watched as his spirit lifted up from his lifeless body. An indescribable bright and magnificent light opened up. As the light came closer, we could see the Savior was the source of the light. He went straight up to Thomas, put His arms around him, and gave him what I would describe as a big bear hug. He kissed him on both cheeks and we could feel a massive flow of love engulf Thomas that went down to his very core. The Savior then took Thomas to the Spirit Prison to await the resurrection and final judgment.

Now, for the rest of the story! Much later in their lives, Evans and Tracy met two sister missionaries and

Overwhelmed by the miracle I had just witnessed, my strength gave out and I sank to my knees. "Do you understand what you have just seen?" Aaron asked me.

Walker knelt down in front of me and said, "I didn't have the words to explain this to you. That is why it was so important for you to come and see for yourself." We were both moved to tears by this experience.

After taking the time to compose ourselves, Aaron again motioned and said, "Look." Before us was Walker's "Fat Man," but I recognized him as Mr. Shoemaker, a man I had met when I was serving as a Bishop. He worked with our LDS Social Services program to help one of our families adopt a baby. He was a wonderful, compassionate, and dedicated man, and I always thought that someday he would join the church. He loved working with families and helping them get their children into the LDS Indian Placement Program. And he loved seeing young people excel as they went through the program.

As we watched, it was easy to see that he was a major advocate for the Smiths when it came to meeting Walker's needs. He pleaded to have Walker's baptism approved. The fight from Indian Affairs, and the red tape he had to deal with on a daily basis within his own agency with regards to Walker, along with his huge case load, finally disheartened him. He made up his mind to leave the program and set up his own private adoption agency.

How ironic that Walker was the pivotal point in motivating all three of these people to change! Mr. Shoemaker, the young girl who rode in the backseat with Walker when he was taken from Kathy and Buddy's home, and Tracy were all moved to better their lives after their confrontation with him. Though Walker intended harm, his actions allowed each to find a new course. His help was what they needed to open the door for the Savior.

Mr. Shoemaker spent his whole life finding good homes for needy children. He was so dedicated to his job that he never married. Many of the deceased family members of the children he had helped were there to greet him the moment he died. Aaron quoted as we looked on, "But Jesus said, 'Suffer little children, and forbid them not, to come unto me: for of such is the kingdom of heaven.'" We looked more closely and saw that the Savior was in the midst of those celebrating Mr. Shoemaker's life.

The scene faded, and we found ourselves sitting back on the cliff overlooking the valley. I was a little amazed to see Aaron sitting there with us. We sat quietly at first watching the subtle shadows change the dimensions of the landscape as the sun worked across the sky. Walker finally commented, "Every judgment I ever made about anyone was totally wrong."

I had to answer him. "Through my life's experiences I've learned that every time I judge someone, if I give them a chance, they frequently change my opinion of them."

Aaron laughed, and again his laugh startled us. "This is the first time I've dealt with a situation like this, and the two of you bring joy to my heart. What a treasured experience this is." The way he worded his statement caused me to wonder if I had died on the trail when I was trying to get back to my car.

Aaron's laughter seemed to ring in our ears and drift through the valley long after our verbal exchange had ended. It drifted on the wind and added depth to the scenery. We watched as a pair of hawks danced together above our heads. Finally Walker spoke up. "Aaron, I know my uncle is okay, but somehow I feel I misjudged that family as well.

Could we see . . . ?" Before he could finish, we were whisked away to the home of Jimmie Begay.

"Look." Walker was scattering the blood all over his bed, walls, and floor. The finishing touch was the bolo tie. Aunt Annie was the first to come into the room. The shock was too much for her and she passed out. She was rushed to the hospital and was treated for a mild heart attack. The police were all over the place. They asked Jimmie to check and see if anything was missing. He was the one who found the blood on the bolo tie.

The officers asked him to come to the station in the morning for questioning and to bring a lawyer with him. Jimmie stood tall and politely told them to ask their questions now because he did not need a lawyer. He was encouraged again to contact his attorney. He told them to do what they needed to do with him but to please not stop looking for Walker because he was certain he was still alive. He was taken to the station and questioned throughout the rest of the night. The next day he offered to take a lie detector test, which he passed. He was well known throughout the community for his integrity, and at least forty people visited him at the station, testifying of his character and volunteering to help in any way they could. After two days, the chief investigator and the district attorney came to the conclusion that this man could never have committed a crime like this, so they sent him home. He was no longer part of the investigation.

Funny, having listened to this story, compared to being an actual witness, reinforced in me one of Walker's major traits: he understates. The room was much worse than I had pictured in my mind. If I didn't already know the story, I would have sworn that a murder had taken place. To the untrained eye, all the evidence pointed to Jimmie, but he had lived his life with such integrity that those who knew him couldn't believe that he would, in any way, be a party to this heinous crime.

It's truly amazing to me that integrity is such a rare commodity these days. I have only known two other people whose lives were defined by it, and I think it's worth a mention here. The first is a man named Lawrence Smith. I once lived in a ward in Bountiful, Utah, for a short time, where almost everyone within the ward boundaries was a member of the LDS church. Everyone was very close. Lawrence was a traveling salesman who was away from home Tuesday through Friday almost every week of the month. I remember his wife receiving a phone call from the police station in Grand Junction, Colorado, telling her that her husband was in jail for driving under the influence and they were going to keep him overnight. She was unable to convince the officer that her husband had to be sick because he would never touch a drink. She called two ladies from the ward who immediately called babysitters, loaded their night cases and pillows into the car, and left for Grand Junction, which was about six hours away. One of the ladies called her husband, a doctor, and asked him to find a doctor in Grand Junction who could meet them at the jail. When they got to Grand Junction, the doctor had already been to the jail and found that Lawrence had kidney failure and was in critical condition. If the doctor hadn't had him taken to the hospital immediately, he would probably have been dead by morning!

I was new in the ward and didn't know the people very well, but what amazed me was that not one person considered for a minute that this man could possibly have taken a drink! He was known for his integrity.

The other man is my grandfather. The family told me he had operated a restaurant in Delta, Colorado, when I was a little boy. As an adult, I had an opportunity to visit the town and wanted to stop at his restaurant while I was there. Where I thought the restaurant had been, there was now a hardware store with a small cafe across the street. I went into the cafe and asked the waitress if she knew anything about a restaurant that had been across the street. I told her I thought my grandfather used to own one there.

An older gentleman sitting at the counter overheard what I was saying. He asked me if my grandfather was Dee Marsh. I told him my grandfather's name was Rex Marsh. He told me he knew a man named Rex who used to go by "Dee." He said he knew a secret about my grandfather that he promised never to tell to anyone, but after all these years he felt someone needed to know. During the depression, my grandfather owned a truck and had hauled produce from Texas to Delta. I believe his name was Earl and he was losing his home to the bank. One night, about 11:00 p.m., my grandfather came to his house and asked him to please come for a ride. Earl was taken to an old white house on Grandpa's property, and inside the house were a variety of food items. Grandpa told him to take enough food to supply his family. While Earl was getting his food, Grandpa went and sat in the truck. Earl was free to take the food he needed without feeling someone was watching what he was taking or judging whether he was taking too much or too little. When my grandfather took Earl back home, the only thing he asked of him was not to say anything to anyone and to please not embarrass him by trying to repay. By the amount of food in the house, Earl suspected my grandfather had helped a large number of other families in that area. He said Grandpa would meet people late at night so no one would be embarrassed about getting help. In those days, any kind of welfare was degrading, embarrassing, disgraceful, and belittling to the men who needed it.

I later stopped by my mom's home and asked her if she knew of a white house near the farm. She told me she did and that it was by the pond on the back acreage. The kids were not allowed to go there. I asked her if she knew if anyone lived there. She told me it was just an old house and that no one used it. I almost told Mom of my experience but decided not to. Only the people Grandpa helped knew what he was doing. If he had wanted her to know, he would have told her. Integrity! You won't find flaxen cords on people like that.

Two or three weeks later after Annie Begay returned home from the hospital, Buddy and Kathy visited her and her family. I felt like I knew Buddy and Kathy intimately, but to see Kathy interact with the Begay family surprised me. Whatever had happened in the past between her family and the Begays was immediately forgotten as she became aware of the desperate situation this family was in. There was no mourning for her lost son as her only thought now was that the Begay family needed her help. Kathy quickly assessed the situation and began organizing the chores in the home. She greeted Aunt Annie with warmth and love and helped her into bed to continue her recovery. She embraced each one of the Begay boys as if they were her own and within hours had the home completely cleaned. It wasn't until dinner was over, the dishes had been done, and the boys were bunked down that any emotion surfaced. She spoke frankly with Jimmie about what had happened and realized that Walker had set this up. She told him she knew Walker was still alive because Robbie had told her that he had had a dream where he saw Walker in his bedroom looking at him. The next morning, when Robbie got up, he noticed that Walker's bedroom door had been opened and all of his dresser drawers had been pulled out. They knew that it had to have been Walker because Walker had always had a problem closing doors and dresser drawers. Kathy called the police and told them why she believed he was still alive and what to look for. The police immediately put out an All-Points Bulletin. Soon after, they received a response from the Montrose County Sheriff's Department that they had a young man fitting Walker's description for a short time, but he ran off and they had not been able to find him.

As I saw how Kathy had put the needs of the Begay family above her own need to be comforted, I found that I was becoming more and more impressed with this remarkable woman.

"Look." We looked and saw that the two families had become close friends. Robbie and the Begay boys split their summers with each family. The Begays owned some scrub Indian ponies, which the boys lived on all summer. The boys had befriended an old Apache who taught them his Apache way to break horses. He told them that an Apache would ride his horse until it died, and then he would cut out the heart and liver and eat them to be one with the animal. The Apache would then catch another wild horse, break it, and keep going. He said that is why the army had such a hard time catching his people. He taught the boys how to tame a horse in one day.

We watched them grow and play together as brothers. The first day school was out every year, Buddy and Kathy took Rob, as he now wished to be called, to stay with the Begays. The boys had made a corral in which they kept water and salt, and when the wild Indian ponies came there, the boys would simply shut the gate and pick out the horses they wanted.

They would snub a horse up to a post and let it fight the post until it exhausted itself. Then they covered the horse's head with a blanket they had slept in the night before so the horse would know their scent. After the horse had calmed down, they hobbled both its front and back legs so the horse couldn't move. With the blanket over its head, the boys would throw a saddle over the horse, crawl all over him, and that night one of them would actually sleep on its back. The next morning they would snub, or tie, the horse to an old horse they called Cowboy. Then they would take the rope hobbles off and replace them with leather straps so the horse would feel like it was still hobbled. With Rob on Cowboy and the other two boys on the unbroken horse, they would ride for many, many miles, gradually letting the wild horse have more and more slack until the horse was on its own. That night, the boy who was breaking the horse would again sleep on the back of the horse whose head was again covered with a blanket.

The next day the boys corralled Cowboy and worked the unbroken horse alone. After the third day, they fed and watered the horse. From that point on, it would follow the boy like a puppy. During the training period they never let the horse lower its head. If it can't lower its head, it can't buck. The boys went through this process with several horses every summer throughout their teenage years. Several times, when they came across a pony herd, one of the horses they had previously broken would leave the herd and spend the rest of the summer following the boys. You can sure learn a lot from an old Apache!

Even though Rob was starting to have difficulty walking, he could sure ride. He felt free of his body and like an eagle floating in the air when he was on a horse. The boys spent up to two weeks at a time on their horses before having to return for supplies. Both families felt that if Rob died out there on a horse, at least he would die happy.

Jimmie took the boys fishing often. They had great fishing trips together, which were very different than the ones they had had with Walker. During the months with the Smiths, the boys attended church with Rob and eventually wanted to be baptized. Jimmie and Annie had long discussions with the Smiths, and after a time they wanted to be baptized also. Nevertheless, they decided not to go ahead because they didn't want to go against the traditions of their people. They did, however, consent to Tommy and Jack joining the church, and Buddy was the one who baptized both boys. Both went on missions, and Tommy was able to bring quite a few families into the church. Jack, on the other hand, worked his heart out and baptized only one family in his first year and two the second year. We watched as these three families flourished and blossomed, and many other families drew closer to Christ because of them.

Walker had suddenly left us, having stepped into the image before us to advise Rob as he prayed with Tommy and Jack. My heart broke as I realized that Walker could have been the fourth boy.

"Aaron, I am so grateful to have the experience of witnessing the beauty and majesty of this place, to watch as Walker forgives himself. Thank you again," I said.

Aaron turned to me and smiled, but his eyes were full of concern. "Bishop, you need to be aware that by being a witness of Heaven your life is in danger."

"I thought perhaps that would be so. Are you able to tell me what to expect?"

A stern furrow crossed his brow, and his smile disappeared. "You will be subject to the lashings of Satan himself, and he will do everything to prevent you from writing down what you are witnessing. You will be locked up and deemed insane. And some will attempt to discredit your words. It will take many years before you will be able to complete your mission and write Walker's life story."

I stood silent for a moment just thinking. Aaron continued, "It is because you have been shown Satan's greatest weapon, and you've witnessed how to defeat it. The knowledge and tools we will give you will be used to defeat the adversary and bind him when the Savior returns to reign on the earth."

"How do I . . . ?" I couldn't formulate the words.

Aaron's countenance lightened again, bringing me peace. "Bishop, the Lord instructed me to bless you with the ability to recount everything you are witnessing. This, I have already told you. Now I bless you with the ability to see each challenge before it happens. You will be able to escape from each attack without harm to your reputation if you trust in the Lord and follow his council as you receive it. You will be instructed through dreams. Trust in what is taught. They will seem random at times, and I bless you with the power of discernment, that the interpretation of each dream will come when you need it." He embraced me. "You will accomplish your mission. I have seen it! Have faith."

Walker returned to join us. "This has been truly amazing! I love this place!"

Aaron laughed again, but this time it didn't startle us. "Walker, my son, this is a place of learning and love. It delights me to know you are enjoying the journey."

Walker's eyes widened. "Aaron, you're one of my grandfathers, aren't you?"

"Yes, from many generations before you were born. My name on earth was Dasan Deen Nahuel, which interpreted means 'Chief Jaguar, God Will Judge.' This is why I am your guide. Families are eternal."

He turned to me and whispered, "My story will be your first dream."

I thought Walker was going to leap out of his skin! He embraced Aaron. "Will I be able to do what you're doing? Be a guide for someone, maybe Tim?"

"As you forgive yourself, you will prepare to be a guide and to have many more assignments."

It seemed like we had visited Aaron and laughed and talked for hours. As we talked, the concern of what was to come melted away, and I found myself at peace with my mission.

Aaron finally turned to Walker and said, "Our time together is not yet complete, but it is time that the Bishop begins his journey. It's time to say goodbye."

CHAPTER 16

THE VISION

The angel looked in my direction, smiling as he left. Walker and I found ourselves on the mesa, once again, looking over the valley as the shadows stretched out like a blanket covering the colors of the day. We stood there meditating on all we had seen. Walker finally spoke and told me that since his spirit had left his body, he would not be able to return. I found the comment peculiar, but realized as I looked at him, that part of accepting life after death was the reality that you cannot return to your old life. I asked Walker how he felt about being dead. This may have been blunt, but I didn't know how else to put it.

Walker reminded me that he knew he was in the Spirit Prison and found it to be a pretty good place. However, he didn't want to stay there. He said he was grateful to have had the opportunity to learn what he had learned, but he knew he had a lot more to learn and wanted to move on.

I had grown to truly love this young man and thought of him as one of my own children. I asked him if there was anything more I could do to help him advance, and I assured him I would do anything he needed me to do. It was then he told me that he had remembered something important as we journeyed through the scenes and visions of his life. He asked me if he could show me a few more things, and of course, I agreed.

Walker bowed his head and spent some time in prayer. When he was finished, the view of his Aunt Annie opened up to us. She was on her knees praying a heartfelt prayer. She was telling God, "Walker is happy where he is and does not want to leave the Smiths." Next to her, Walker's real mom and dad whispered to her, "Walker is needed on the reservation and you should do everything you can to bring him home." When she told this to Uncle Jimmie, he told her he would do everything he could, but he didn't really have the heart for it because he knew Walker didn't want to leave his foster family. Since Jimmie never doubted anything Aunt Annie received in her prayers, he used his influence with the tribe to initiate the process to bring Walker home. His uncle's attorney, who Walker had hated so much, did all of his work at a discounted rate as a favor to them. He had once tried to marry Annie and still cared very much for her. Walker remarked, "You have to love them because they never gave up and never stopped trying!"

I asked Walker why it was so important for him to go back to the reservation and he reminded me of the baptism talk he was supposed to have given at Bart's and Bobbie's baptism. He said that, as he had been prayerfully preparing the talk, he realized that he'd been called to deliver his people from the bondage of the false traditions of their fathers. And return to the traditions of the ancient ones whose history is found in the Book of Mormon. He was certain that if he had delivered the gospel message in his talk, Bart would have taken it not only to the reservation but also to Russia where his company had sent him on his next job assignment. As a result of this message of hope, millions of lives would ultimately have been affected. These millions would have taught many more about the Savior and His Plan of Salvation or Plan of Happiness as it is also known, which would have freed them from Satan's cords. "Satan knew I was the one who would have the powerful knowledge which would spell the beginning of the end of his reign here on earth. He was determined to destroy me before I could share this information with anyone, and I played right into his hands," explained Walker.

Walker spoke often of the visions he had had and the knowledge he had received, and I had already been warned that my life would be in peril because of it. I now wondered if Walker had given me all the information he wanted me to know. I had thought his message was all about faith, forgiveness, and the false traditions of our forefathers, but now I felt that that wasn't the case. "Walker, have you told me everything you want me to know yet?"

A great smile broadened his face. "No. No, I guess I haven't. We talked about many things, but we never got to it. Are you sure you want to know?" He waited to see the expression on my face. I must have responded to his liking because he let out a laugh. "Your face speaks volumes, my friend."

A seriousness came over Walker as he realized the direction his life had gone and how Satan had tried to destroy him after he had received this information. "You must understand, Bishop, that once I share everything with you, Satan will do whatever he can to destroy you as he did me."

Walker knelt beside me and looked intently into my face. "My brother, you will not bear this burden alone. This is my promise to you." As penetrating as his truthful stare had been, his reassuring words also spoke to my soul. They gave me hope. "I'm ready to hear what you have to tell me," I said.

A brightness surrounded us as Aaron rejoined us. We decided to sit at the edge of the mesa as we talked. "As I studied for Bart's baptismal talk, I wanted it to be as special to him as he was to me. Bart had already told me that he knew for sure the Book of Mormon was the word of God, so I had a solid base upon which to start my research. I was studying about faith and repentance, and I don't know why I turned to the words in Alma, chapter 30, verses 30 through 44 in the Book of Mormon. It was the story of Korihor, an antichrist, who demanded a sign from the Lord before he would declare the scriptures to be true. Alma, the chief judge and governor over all the land, told him, 'Thou hast had signs enough; will ye tempt your God?'

"As I read these verses, I heard a calm voice speaking to me saying, 'Here is the information you need for your research. Mother Earth will bear her own testimony of Elohim.' I looked around to see where the voice came from, but no one was there."

Walker looked over to Aaron. "It was you, wasn't it?"

"Yes," said Aaron. "You wanted to know how to find the pure truth, and because you asked, I was able to guide and direct you."

Walker continued. "Alma told Korihor he already had the testimony of all the holy prophets, his brethren, the scriptures, and all those things denote there is a God. Even the earth and all things that are upon the face of it, its motion, and also the planets which move in their regular form witness there is a Supreme Creator.

"I realized how important this information was, so I wrote it all down. I was pleased with myself because I knew my people believed the earth could talk and reveal things to them.

"I thought more about what I needed to do next. As I pondered and prayed, the next prompting came, 'Search the words of wise men and learn from their experiences. Learn from all thy brethren.'

"I turned to another interesting story from the Book of Mormon about Lehi, a dying prophet, who called his children together to give each of them a last blessing. He said his lineage went back to Joseph who was carried captive into Egypt. He said God promised Joseph of Egypt He would raise up a great prophet in the last days. He said the prophet's name would be Joseph, and the prophet's father's name would also be Joseph. He said this prophet would be great like unto Moses 2 Neph: 3: 3-12, take a close look at verse 9.

"I decided to put this prophecy from the Book of Mormon to the test. I wanted to see if I could identify this prophet by scripture and have the earth act as a second witness.

"The only religious leader I could think of whose name was Joseph and whose father's name was also Joseph was Joseph Smith Jr, the first prophet and president of The Church of Jesus Christ of Latter-day Saints.

"I found some interesting comparisons. Moses had Aaron for a spokesman because he had difficulty speaking. Joseph Smith had Oliver Cowdrey act as scribe for him because he was weak in writing. Moses and Joseph both used the Urim and Thummim to communicate with God. Moses performed miracles and prophesied of signs and wonders. Joseph did the same. Moses led the people from Egypt. Joseph led the people from Ohio to Missouri and prepared them for their journey to the West. Moses wasn't allowed to enter the Promised Land. Joseph tried to escape to the West, but God sent him back to Missouri. Sometime later, Joseph was killed, so like Moses, he never entered the Promised Land. If Joseph had gone to the Promised Land, in Utah, Lehi's prophecy would not fit Joseph and my test would have failed. Both men were directed by God to teach the people His laws and ordinances and establish his priesthood to help them draw closer to Him. Moses had the Tabernacle where God dwelled, and Joseph built temples for God.

"I found these few comparisons more than interesting, and there are many more comparisons if you look for them. Again, a voice whispered to me and told me, 'So far, so good, but by law truth requires more than one witness, check with the earth.' I wondered what that meant.

"I put a lot of thought into this, and guess what I found? The only two places on earth where there are dead seas are in Israel and in Utah. Also, God, working through the US politicians of that day, created Utah in the shape of the ancient symbol of the covenant, which is a square with one corner removed. This shows that God made a covenant with his people, not only in Israel, but also in Utah, just as the Prophet Lehi stated in 2 Nephi, chapter 3 in the Book of Mormon. He used the earth to give His proof. For those who seek, and for those who ask, this is how 'the Lord gives understanding in all things'" (2 Timothy 2:7).

Aaron patiently stood by, but unlike Walker, his countenance was much more sober. "Walker, tell Bishop what happened next," he said.

"Bishop, as I sat pondering my vision, I realized that pure truth is unshakable when you have the testimony of the Ancient Ones, the scriptures, the prophets, and the earth all testifying that what you are seeking is true. I found that all of these things testify that Joseph Smith was a true prophet of God." It was at that point I noticed a dark presence enter my room. As it started moving toward me, I desperately wanted to run but I was unable to move. Negative thoughts began to fill my head I wasn't able to be baptized; I wasn't able to have the priesthood; those evil people were trying to take me away from my mom and my family; Scotty, my best friend, was dead because God had ignored my pleas for him to be healed! I felt myself becoming angry and resentful, even hateful, and I knew that before long I would succumb to the will of this evil presence. Just then, Mom came into the room, and the darkness dispersed as if it was afraid to face her. I felt a dark cloud hanging over me for some time after that. Looking back, I now realize that that experience was also a testament to me that Joseph Smith Jr was a prophet because the same thing happened to him in the Sacred Grove. He went there to find truth, and a dark presence descended upon him. Evil conspired to stop Joseph from finding truth, which was exactly what was happening to me! I thought I would be destroyed before I could tell anyone what I had learned in my vision. When I came up here onto the mesa, I cried out a desperate and heartfelt prayer hoping that God would see fit to save me from the darkness. The next thing I knew, you were there, Bishop. You were the answer to my prayer. Now I know my people will be saved from the false traditions of their fathers."

I felt the divine power he spoke of as he testified to me of the lessons he had learned by using the formula made known to him for finding pure truth. I knew that Satan would do everything in his power to destroy Walker's message because Satan has no defense against pure truth. The weight of knowing what I now knew was heavy to bear until Aaron put his arm around me and said, "Bishop, don't forget. You will never be alone."

I thought about two boys robbing a bank, a man framed for murder, and Nita, the way tragedy had struck her not only once but twice! I thought of Tadi's tragic death as he made his way down the mountain trail with his pack horses! If I hadn't seen for myself, how all of this fit into Heavenly Father's plan and all of the miracles that had been accomplished with just one life, I wouldn't have believed any of this. I fell to my knees and prayed for the strength I would need to carry out this sacred mission.

Aaron explained to me that since I was going into battle and needed protection, he would be honored if I would take his shield with me. Aaron told me that he had fought in many battles, and to be able to take possession of the shield of this great warrior was more than I had ever hoped for. Aaron told me Jacob 1:4 was on his shield to let his enemies know who and what kind of person they were facing. As he handed me the shield, I could see the scripture engraved upon it. I was ashamed to admit it, but I didn't know this scripture and had to ask Aaron if he would recite it. Aaron quoted Jacob 1:4 from the Book of Mormon, "And if there were preaching which was sacred, or revelation which was great, or prophesying, that I should engraven the heads of them upon these plates, and touch upon them as much as it were possible, for Christ's sake, and for the sake of our people." He added, "You will also need a breastplate and helmet."

I told Aaron I also wanted my breastplate to be made of the scriptures. Walker said, "If that's what you want, Aaron and I will help you develop it." Walker also told me that the more I knew about the scriptures, the more influence I would have in other people's lives.

Aaron went on to state that his era was about seventy-five years before the birth of the Savior. He had told us earlier that on this earth he was known as Dasan Deen Nahuel, which interpreted means "Chief Jaguar, God Will Judge." He said that in his day, their history was recorded by drawing the profiles of their faces and writing their history on their helmets or head dresses. He said that my history would also be written on my helmet.

Aaron said, "Bishop, we used this form of writing to decorate our helmets, breastplates, and shields to warn our enemies of who they were facing."

To understand what it means to have our history written on our heads, you need to understand our form of writing. It was a form of poetry or a rhetorical inversion of the second of two parallel structures. They would take a subject, and starting at one end they would tell a story. At the end of the story, they used the statement, or sometimes the first letter of each line, to tell another story, which would go from the end back to the beginning. At first, I didn't have any idea what he was talking about. He called it chiasmus writing and gave me an example.

He started with line A: "He is a worry to his father." Line A tells what the son is to his father. Underneath line A, he writes, B: "He is a foolish son." Line B tells why he is a worry to his father. Then going back up and across from line A is line Aa: "And bitterness to her-who-bore-him." Line Aa takes you back to the beginning but talks about the mother and how the son affects her.

A. He is a worry to his father. Aa. And bitterness to her-who-bore him.

B. He is a foolish son.

I told him I thought I understood. "Do you have another example to clarify it even more?"

Aaron replied, "I have an example that you can take to the Indian nations, and they will understand." Aaron stooped and began writing in the dirt. He wrote Joseph Smith Jr's name starting with the *J* at the top and going down to the last letter, which is *R*. Then he reversed the spelling placing the *R* at the bottom and the *J* at the top. It ended up in a V shape. He reminded Walker and me that it will not work unless you use Joseph's full name, which is Joseph Smith Jr. It was done this way so that God could show man that he chose Joseph to be his prophet. God used the letters in Joseph's name to tell His story about Joseph and Joseph's calling on this earth.

There in the dirt he wrote **JosephSmithJr** and **rJhtimShpesoJ**. It looked like this:

J. Jesus   J. justified

O. opens	O. ordinances
S. seals	S. sealing
E. engravings	E. endowments
P. prophet	P. priesthood
H. has	H. holy
S. seen	S. sacred
M. Moroni	M. making
I. introducing	I. in
T. the	T. teacher
H. heavenly	H. honored
J. joyous	J. Joseph
R. restoration	R. rendering

There it was before us, Joseph's purpose and accomplishments on earth written in his name or on his head. Aaron quoted another scripture, Matthew 13:16: "But blessed are your eyes for they see: and your ears, for they hear." Aaron said that I should have the Book of Mormon inscribed on my breastplate. Now I wrote in the dirt, filling in the words after writing the letters, **thebookofmormon** and **nomromfokoobeht.**

T. truth	T. translated
H. has	H. had
E. emerged	E. El (God the Father)
B. by	B. book
O. opening	O. only
O. our	O. of
K. knowledge	K. knowledge
O. of	O. opening
F. future	F. for
M. missionary	M. miracle
O. opportunities	O. ongoing
R. regarding	R. revelations
M. more	M. making
O. open	O. opportunities
N. nations	N. new

He also said Lehi's ancestry went all the way back to Joseph who was a slave in Egypt. As such, Lehi was raised in Egypt and became a very wealthy trader in Jerusalem. He had the learning of the Jews and the language of the Egyptians. (1 Nephi 1:2). He pointed out that the name Mormon comes from two Egyptian words. Mor = love, Mon = eternal or everlasting. Or you might say The Book of Love Everlasting

I sat and pondered the words in the dirt. What really caught my attention was that more nations would be opened up to missionary work with the Book of Mormon being used as the cornerstone. I was seeing God's hand in this work in a way I had never imagined before.

I noticed a sadness come over Walker as we worked together in the dirt. His voice quivered as he said, "Bishop, if I hadn't been influenced by the promptings of the Evil One, this knowledge would have sent me down different paths. I could have been instrumental in saving many from the bonds of Satan and bringing millions unto Christ."

"Walker, my son, do not be dismayed by what you did not accomplish. I know you believe that you were the messenger of truth for Bart and Bobbie, and that you failed with your mission on earth. However, there is something I saw in your lean-to that has become clear to me through the explanation of chiasmus. Bart knew about chiasmus before you even knew what it was."

Walker looked at me with a quizzical look. "How do you know?"

"Would you review the part of your life when Bart made the bag for your eagle feather?"

Walker immediately bowed in prayer, and the scene opened before us of Bart making the leather pouch. He inscribed something on the inside of the leather. We gave it close inspection and noticed a chiasmus.

"Walker, the chiasmus is of the Bible. As you lay comatose before your passing, I saw your eagle feather and held it, hoping by doing so I would feel better. I noticed the markings tooled into the leather when I looked inside. Bart knew you would somehow understand its meaning."

As the scene continued, we saw Bobbie enter the room where Bart was working the leather. "Why are you doing that?" she asked playfully.

Bart was calm but serious with his answer. "This next week is important to me. I get the feeling Walker needs my guidance and help through some bad times. And I'm sad that I have to tell him we're leaving. I want to give him every tool I can."

"What are you writing on the leather?" asked Bobbie.

"I'm adding something called chiasmus to the inside of the leather. I hope he will see and understand its value. Many people will attempt to discredit the truth found in the Bible. I know we communicate with God through prayer, but He communicates with us through the Bible. The Bible leads us to the knowledge that Jesus is the Christ, Creator of the World, Redeemer, and Savior of mankind. As Walker studies the chiasmus, I want him to understand that no matter what his question is, or what the problems he might be facing, the answer can be found in the Bible.

Bart inscribed these letters on the leather: Bible spelled forward and spelled backward.

"God also wrote his sermon on the he ad of the Bible."
BIBLE (spelled backward) ELBIB

B. (basic)

I. (instruction)

B. (before)

L. (leaving)

E. (earth)

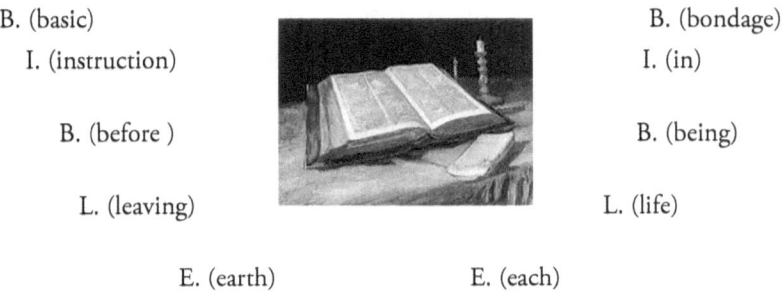

B. (bondage)

I. (in)

B. (being)

L. (life)

E. (each)

"You see, Walker, Bart was guided through his life to understand the message when it came. He already understood how to find truth. Your message was for you, more than for Bart. He knew the Bible was only one witness and could not release people from Satan's bondage by itself."

Aaron said, "You need two or more witnesses so the prophets can tell the full story. The Bible is the witness of Jesus Christ on the eastern hemisphere, which is known as the stick of Judah, and the Book of Mormon is the witness of Jesus Christ on the western hemisphere, known as the stick of Joseph (Ezekiel 37:15–17). The Bible testifies of Jesus and the apostasy, and the Book of Mormon testifies of Jesus and living prophets. The Bible leads you to Jesus Christ, and the Book of Mormon leads you to Jesus and the eternal and sacred ordnances that can only be performed in temples. "

Aaron opened to a scene where Moses and other high priests were going into the Tabernacle. I saw angels descending from the heavens entering into the Tabernacle and coming out with what looked like gold cards. They then went to the gates of Paradise where messengers were waiting for their return. The messengers took the cards into the Spirit Prison and met with the persons whose names were on the cards and taught them about the Savior and what was required for them to be able to leave the Spirit Prison and go into Paradise. They were able to choose whether or not to accept the teachings. If they accepted the teachings, the cards became golden keys, which allowed them to pass through the gates of Paradise. The Spirit Prison was full of people waiting for the cards.

The scene changed, and we came upon a city that had been destroyed because of the extreme wickedness of the people. Satan was there. All the people who had been destroyed were so bound down with flaxen cords they looked like they were in cocoons. Satan laughed as he watched them make their way into the Spirit Prison.

As we looked on, what was happening in the Spirit Prison reminded me of the process by which a caterpillar becomes a butterfly. The process starts with the caterpillar, a destructive little worm, but in the cocoon it is transformed into a beautiful butterfly. The people were told that because of their wickedness they had been captured by Satan and had to go into the Spirit Prison. However, under the Savior's plan, they could change their lives and accept the Savior and the Father's plan of justice and mercy. Like the butterfly leaving the cocoon, those accepting the Savior would be able to leave their cords behind and return into Heavenly Father's presence, that is, change from destructive man (caterpillar) into a Christ like son (beautiful butterfly).

Again, the scene changed, and we could see temples scattered all over the earth. From all these temples I could see angels taking gold cards to the Spirit Prison, creating holes of light through the cocoons surrounding the multitudes Satan had bound. Every time an angel entered with a gold card, Satan would go into a rampage. He fought openly to destroy the temples by sending people he could control to pollute them. Once a temple was polluted, the angels were no longer able to enter. We witnessed the history of the earth as temple after temple was destroyed. We came to Herod's temple, in Jerusalem, and watched as Satan polluted it by using the flaxen cords of tradition to taint the truth taught inside. Jesus cleansed it and the angels once again were able to bring gold cards from the temple. In a rage, Satan had the temple destroyed and succeeded in having all the apostles and prophets with priesthood authority from the Father killed. No one was left to fulfill the work in the temples, and there were no cards to be taken to the Spirit Prison. Satan laughed again at his accomplishments, mocking God. He controlled the world.

The scene continued as choice spirits started descending from heaven to earth. The scriptures were kept from the people because they were written in languages most people could not understand. These choice spirits had freedom written on their hearts and could not be comforted without the Word of God. As they rebelled against traditions that Satan had tainted, they were made to suffer unspeakable hardships, and some gave their lives to create access to the scriptures. I had studied about the reformers, but to actually see what they had gone through was horrifying. I esteem these men and women as some of the greatest spirits to have ever come to the earth.

Though Satan used every effort to stifle and crush truth, he couldn't stop the scriptures from coming forth.

Nevertheless, he was not to be defeated easily. As the Bible was translated, Satan influenced scribes to change passages to appeal to their sense of vanity and tradition. Satan thought he could destroy God's work by using man's weaknesses, but truth cannot be altered or hidden.

Aaron explained, "To counter the efforts of Satan, God put packets of light which illuminate the mind with wisdom, understanding, and truth on every page. Because truth is on the pages, the Bible can be used as a direct line of communication with God. If you have a problem or question, you can go to the Bible and God will use the packets of light to enlighten you with knowledge and wisdom far beyond your years. You will know He is there."

The scene closed and Walker and I were again sitting on the cliff overlooking the valley below. Walker turned to me and said, "With the scriptures as your breastplate, Satan will not be able to get to your heart."

I asked if my two-edged sword could be the words of the prophets, and Aaron enthusiastically replied, "Wise choice, Bishop. The gentiles have embraced the secret combinations and will soon be completely surrounded by sin. Up until the present time, the prophets have been warning about Gadianton robbers, secret combinations, and perverted forms of governments, and calling for the people to repent. Now they are admonishing the people not only to repent but also to prepare for what is coming. The prophecy in 3 Nephi, chapter 16, in the Book of Mormon, is in the process of being fulfilled. It is now time for the Native American people to join with the Lord's prophet to prepare for the Second Coming of the Lord, Jesus Christ."

We were startled to see Aaron step off the edge of the cliff and stand before us in midair. In his hand was a gold card. "Walker, you have spent your life creating your name. Now it is time for your Heavenly Father to give you a new name. Your name will be changed to Bemossed-Cheveyo-Qaletaga, which in Hopi means 'Walker, Spirit Warrior, and Guardian of the People.'" Walker accepted this information with his usual humility and grace.

"You are Bemossed because you will walk with those who need help in locating their ancestors so the temple work can be done for them. You are also Cheveyo because you have fought the good fight, and Qaletaga because you will go and help save those in the Spirit Prison. Come, let us go to the gates of Paradise."

Bemossed turned to me and gave me a great big smile, which warmed my heart. "I shall also be your guardian. It's in my name." And with that, he walked toward the sunlight, which was rising brilliantly above the valley, his gold card in hand. Tearfully, I watched as Bemossed disappeared into the light.

Aaron startled me again by placing his hand on my shoulder. "Your time here is complete. But before you go back to your life and mission, there is one thing more you should see."

Aaron told me Walker was baptized but still needed to have his temple ordinances done. Jack did those for him vicariously. Walker could now go to the Spirit Prison and teach Dibe Yazhi (Little Lamb), the gospel. She was the girl Walker tried to rescue in the cabin but she was already dead. They had been best friends in the pre-existence before they came to earth. She accepted Jesus Christ's Gospel so he brought her to Paradise. Now her temple work could be done and they could be married and sealed together for time and all eternity. Buddy represented Walker, and Kathy represented Dibe Yazhi, acting as proxies in this ceremony, and now they were married and sealed together for time and all eternity.

Walker could also now go into the Sprit Prison to get Tim. Tim was in a very dark and dangerous place. Walker didn't care, he went there anyway. Tim accepted what we call the Gospel of Jesus Christ and Walker brought Tim out of that dark and horrible place into the Light. Tim is now Walker's very best friend.

Tadi and Nita later were baptized and had their temple ordnances done for them. Buddy and Kathy were married and sealed for them. Now, Walker could be sealed to them as their son and Jack had the honor of representing Walker for that sealing. Bringing families together and binding them together for all time and eternity is one of the main tenets of Heavenly Father's plan.

You may think this was the end of Walker's story but it was just beginning. Heavenly Father and Jesus Christ sent both families into the Spirit Prison to teach the Gospel to thousands upon thousands of their ancestors so they would have the choice to either accept or reject Jesus Christ's saving ordnances. If you want to know what great missionary couples are like, those are two wonderful and powerful examples.

"Look." We viewed Satan being told of Walker's conquest. Pure rage and hate poured from him as the news of the warrior's triumph was heralded. Then he stopped and looked straight at me. His eyes were cold and frightening. "We'll meet soon," he said. "On earth I stopped him and I will stop you too." The scene closed and we were back on the mesa.

"Satan knows he could not stop the scriptures from going forth, or temples from being built. He has no weapon that can defeat pure truth. His only victory will come from destroying as many of the sons and daughters of God as he can. His followers will aid him in inflicting as much damage as possible. They will use 'social justice,' which is actually social injustice, 'economic equality' to punish the producers and enslave the poor through government handouts, 'collective salvation' to make everyone like bricks, even though each individual is unique and responsible for his or her own personal life and salvation, complacency, debt, environmental programs, many of which are used to control almost every aspect of people's lives, propaganda, political correctness and racism to manipulate the people and to take over governments, churches, and charities. Satan's followers will use the passion of the terrorist to take peace from the earth and destroy the lives of millions. Satan will use religion to murder innocent women and children, having them believe they do it in God's name. He will destroy governments, and anarchy will reign so he can corrupt the minds of simple men with irreverent thought. Shortages of food will be used to create riots and chaos, and in that chaos he will capture millions of souls. Satan will become so brazen that he will no longer keep his intentions secret. He will send an Antichrist to enslave the weak-minded and to control all nations, and the governments of those nations will be responsible for the deaths of many millions of their citizens. This is your warning, Bishop. By these methods, even the most elect of God can be deceived.

"Satan also has followers in the Spirit Prison. Even though pure truth is the reigning light in the hereafter, some will reject the message of hope because of their free will. Others, like Bemossed, understand the horror and pain from the devil's reign of terror. They will have greater appreciation for the Father's plan because they have experienced the bitter fruits of wickedness and the joys of righteousness. Satan may triumph on the earth for a short time, but soon the Lord will return. And, because of the righteousness of the people, Satan will be bound."

Aaron took me by the shoulder and led me away from the cliff and back toward the lean-to. "You are one of God's elect, foreordained to fulfill this mission. If you listen closely, you will hear me and Bemossed whisper the truth of each situation. You are not alone." He embraced me. "There is one more thing you need to know before you return. The Hopis will become spiritual leaders working with God's prophets, and the Cheyenne, as well as most other tribes, will become His representatives serving as foot soldiers with the gentiles to bring His righteous sons and daughters back to the Father. However, before the tribes can do this, they must embrace the formula for finding pure truth. Also they must lay down the false traditions of their fathers and take up the true traditions of the ancient ones. Our Father has already prepared children who will come to the earth to teach them.

With this I found myself on my back gazing skyward outside of Walker's lean-to. The night of his death had passed, and although it felt like I had been gone for months, only a few short moments had passed. I stood up and went into the lean-to. Walker's body was emaciated and shrunken, totally different from Bemossed's true frame. He had truly used up his body during his short life.

My heart felt heavy as I picked him up and carried him to the tomb he had hollowed out of sandstone in one of the large crevasses. I went back to his camp and gathered up all of his worldly belongings and placed them in the tomb with him so he would have easy access to them in the afterlife. Then I proceeded to take off the clothing he was wearing and dressed him in his breechclout. I cut his hair in the Hopi style, which is shoulder length with straight cut bangs. The Hopi cut their hair this way to represent looking through a window for the coming of God. Finally, I placed a leather band around his forehead, preparing him for when the eagles crown him with their feathers. In his hands, I placed his quiver, medicine bag, and the eagle feather Bart had prepared for him. I spent the rest of the day walling up the tomb with the rocks Walker had gathered for that purpose. I dedicated his tomb and, in prayer, thanked God for my time with him.

The daylight was fleeting as I climbed back up onto the mesa. I looked toward the great nest of Walker's eagle and knelt down upon my knees, raising my arms into the air and calling Great Dyami (Great Soaring Eagle) to come take Walker's spirit to God. The huge bird rose from the nest, dropped close to the ground and down through the crevasses. When he reached the area of Walker's tomb, he caught an updraft and went straight up into the sky. I watched until Dyami completely disappeared out of sight.

"An impressive sight, isn't it?" To my surprise someone was sitting on the edge of the mesa in the same location where Walker and I had spent so much time. At first glance I thought I knew him and I started to call out, but stopped, sensing the evil before me. The individual turned and looked at me. Cocking his head and patting the rock beside him, he motioned for me to come and sit beside him. I recognized him from the vision I had before I returned. It was Satan himself.

I told him I was aware of his treachery and that I would not be distracted from my mission.

Two others emerged from the shadows that I recognized as Othman Wecksler and Saif al Din, both close friends and business associates of my son's. Satan was there in his spirit form, but Othman and

Saif were living sons of God who had been completely corrupted by Satan because they had followed his evil influence. I knew them to be powerful and dangerous men.

One more man stepped from behind the great stone that was part of Walker's lean-to. My heart leaped when I saw that the man was my son, Asher, who was one of the main reasons I had come up onto this mesa. I had felt a need to ask God for special help in guiding him back from his evil ways.

As I stood in shock at seeing my son there, Othman and Saif grabbed me and bound me with strong leather cords. I looked to my son for aid, but he just looked at me and grinned. As he moved next to Satan, I could see that there was no hope that he would help me out of my predicament. I looked into Satan's eyes, and I could see the whole earth in chaos with these three men at the head, having caused all the conditions leading to the chaos. They would become known as the Antichrist. I could see Satan trying to hide something. I looked deeper into his eyes, and I saw the Latter-day Saints and all the good people on the earth going to selected gathering places throughout the world for their protection. I recognized one of these gathering places as the three sacred Hopi mesas. The Antichrist and their followers could not touch the people or do them any harm because of their righteousness.

I called to my son and said, "Stand by me. Satan will be leaving here shortly." Instead of moving toward me, he hid behind Satan, and Satan just laughed.

With knives in hand, Othman and Saif came toward me intending to slit my throat, but before they could carry out their evil deed, I heard a whisper, saying, "Use your priesthood."

"Touch me not!" I said in a commanding voice. "You shall have no power over me!" The cords by which I was bound slid from my wrists. "Satan, Othman, Saif, and Asher, in the name of Jesus Christ and by the power of the Holy Melchizedek Priesthood, I command you to depart." Suddenly, a mighty wind blew from above and forced Satan off the cliff. Othman, Saif, and Asher scrambled from the mesa down into the crevasses and were quickly out of sight.

I could hear my son's shrill voice calling through the darkness, "It's better to rule in hell than to serve in heaven."

I knew another great battle had just begun. I spent the next few hours thanking God and dedicating the mesas as holy ground. Though my heart was greatly saddened by seeing my son hide behind Satan, one thought gave me great relief. I was not alone.

Aaron whispered to me, "Now that you have dedicated these mesas as holy ground, they will become a place of refuge and safety, a place for you to come and heal from the many wounds you will suffer. Evil will never be able to come here and harm you."

I now had all the ammunition I needed, thanks to Walker. Looking to heaven, I raised my arms and cried out, "I'm ready!" "Bring it on!"

Is Joseph Smith Truly God's Prophet in the Latter Days?

Over the years, I have had many people tell me they know a lot of members of The Church Of Jesus Christ of Latter-Day Saints and they just love them because they are good friends and neighbors. They are recognizing we are Christians not only by the name of our Church, but also by the way we live. They love the way our Church is organized and how we take care of our own people. When there is a disaster, we are often called upon to organize crews to help with clean-up and provide food and clothing. They often say they can accept everything about us except Joseph Smith and modern-day living prophets.

For me, it was the other way around. I couldn't accept the other churches because they didn't have prophets. A few of them said they had prophets but they couldn't tell me where those prophets got their authority, and that didn't feel right to me. When the missionaries started teaching me about Joseph Smith and how the Father and the Son personally called him to be the prophet in these latter days, I knew that that was just what I was looking for.

The missionaries who were teaching me about the church asked me to read Moroni 10:3 in the Book of Mormon which says, "Behold, I would exhort you that when ye shall read these things, if it be the wisdom in God that ye shall read them, that ye would remember how merciful the Lord had been unto the children of men, from the creation of Adam even down until the time that ye shall receive those things, and ponder it in your hearts." **(The first thing I needed to understand was that it was wisdom in God for me to be introduced to the Book of Mormon or I wouldn't be having that experience. The second thing I needed to do was to ponder those things which means I had to do more than just read the book).**

Moroni 10:4 goes on to state, "And when ye shall receive these things, I would exhort you that ye would ask God, the Eternal Father, in the name of Christ, if these things **are not** true. (**Because of God's wisdom I had this book, so I needed to assume it was true. I also needed to ask Him which part of it was not true knowing that He keeps His promises and would let me know what was true. I couldn't find anything that was not true).**

Moving on in Moroni 10:4, it states, "and if ye ask with a sincere heart, with real intent," (**Having a sincere heart means that I am not playing games. I really want to know. Real intent means if you let me know it is true I will do whatever the Savior requires of me. Understanding it means being baptized by His Priesthood holder who has the authorized authority).**

"Having faith in Christ, he will manifest the truth of it unto you, by the power of the Holy Ghost." This is a simple test as to whether the Book of Mormon is true or not.

As I was doing research for my book "The Healing of Windwalker: A Story of Love, Hate and Redemption", the Lord, pointed out some very interesting facts to me. He showed me how the Book of Mormon prophesied, and even named Joseph as the Latter-day prophet in a way that cannot be duplicated by man.

The Book of Mormon is the religious history of a family that God led out of Jerusalem before Nebuchadnezzar destroyed Jerusalem in the days when Zedekiah was king. He led Lehi and his family to North America and were the progenitors of many of the Native Americans who settled the North Eastern area around what is called the American Heartland. 3 Nephi, chapters 10-30 tell of Christ's visit to them after his Resurrection which is very interesting and informative.

So, how does the Book of Mormon prophesy, in an undeniable way, that Joseph Smith was a prophet?

Heavenly Father sets patterns so it is easier for us to understand His dealings with man. For example, in Deu. 18:18-22, God tells Moses in verse 18, "I will raise them up a Prophet from **among their brethren,** like unto thee, and will put my words in his mouth; and he shall speak into them all that I shall command him." (**"Among their brethren" is speaking of the prophet who will be raised up to the Jews which** was Jesus Christ. Like Moses delivered Israel from Egypt, Christ will deliver them from sin and death.

In the Book of Mormon, Alma 30:41-45, explains how God give us signs about Joseph Smith.

In this chapter Korihor, the antichrist, ridicules Christ, the Atonement, and the Spirit of Prophecy. He teaches that there is no God, no fall of man, no penalty for sin, and no Christ. His teachings led many people astray so he was taken to Alma the High Priest for judgment. Alma testifies that Christ shall come and **that all things denote there is a God.**

Let's take a close look at Alma 30:44 and see how Alma explains how all things denote there is a God when Korihor asks Alma to give him a sign. But Alma says unto him; thou has had signs enough; will ye tempt your God? Will ye say, show unto me a sign, <u>when ye have the testimony of all these thy brethren,</u> **(this means the testimony of all the members of the church)** and all the holy prophets? **He is talking about the ancient as well as modern prophets).** <u>The scriptures are laid before thee,</u> (meaning both the Bible and Book of Mormon), and all things denote there is a God; yea even <u>the earth and all things that are upon the face of it,</u> **(God will use the earth and all things upon it because this is something man cannot manipulate)** yea, and its motion, yea and also all the planets which move in their regular form do witness that there is a supreme Creator.

Korihor insisted on a sign and God gave him one. He struck him dumb. Korihor admitted there was a Supreme Creator and that the Devil had deceived him by appearing as an angel and taught him the things he was teaching to the people. Because of this, He lost his voice and all his wealth. He became a beggar and was run over by the people and killed. Where was the Devil? He was laughing at how we destroyed Korihor!

<u>Let's use this formula:</u>

1. When ye have the testimony of all these thy brethren
2. Scriptures are laid before thee
3. All the holy prophets
4. Earth and all things that are upon the face of it

5.   All the planets which move in their regular orbits

1. The testimony of all these thy brethren

1.   Let's start with the <u>testimony of the brethren</u>. In the introduction to the Book of Mormon you have the eyewitness testimony. I can add my testimony to theirs because I have put in a lot of study and prayers and received my witness from the Holy Ghost.

2. Scriptures are laid before thee

2.   Let's continue in the Book of Mormon and see how the Lord used the scriptures to identify Joseph Smith. In 2 Nephi, Lehi was on his deathbed and giving his children his final blessings. Chapter 3 is very interesting because it gives details about a prophet and Seer who will be raised up on this content in the latter days. The whole chapter is important so please read it in full. In verse 4, Lehi says he is a descendant of Joseph who was carried captive into Egypt, and that Joseph saw Lehi's day. In verse 6, Joseph says that a seer will be raised up out of Lehi's lineage. Verse 9 states that the seer would be great like unto Moses. Verse 12 says that <u>Lehi's record</u>, i.e., **The Book of Mormon** will be combined with the record of **Judah** to grow together to confound false doctrine **(Compare Ezekiel 37:15-19).** In Verse 15, Joseph of Egypt says the Seer's Name would be Joseph after his name, and also Joseph after his father's name which would make the Seer Joseph Smith, Jr.

3. All The Holy Prophets

3. Ezekiel 37:15-19 tells about the stick (or record) of Judah (the Bible) and the Stick of Joseph (which is in the hand of Ephraim or the Book of Mormon) joined together to become one in our hand.

Revelation 14:16 says in the last days John saw "another angel fly in the midst of heaven, having the everlasting gospel to preach unto them that dwell on the earth, and to every nation, and kindred, and tongue, and people.

We know this angel as the "Angel Moroni" found on top of all the temples of The Church of Jesus Christ of Latter-Day Saints.

Let's put 2 Nephi 3:10-15 to the test and see how Joseph Smith Jr. is like unto Moses

As I was studying this chapter the Spirit told me to pay special attention to 2 Nephi 3:9 and compare Joseph Smith Jr. to see how he is like unto Moses. I did that and what I found was truly amazing!

Moses: was born to Levi a Levite (Ws. 2:1

Moses: saw Jehovah (Jesus Christ) and talked with him (Ex. 24:9-11) (Numbers 12:5-8)

Moses: worked signs and wonders for the first time since Israel's captivity in Egypt (Ex. 7:10)

Moses: organizes the church (Ex. 18)

Moses: used the Urim & Thummin (Ex. 38)

Moses: received the 10 commandments as well as the other commandments (Ex. 19 etc.)

Moses: Aaron was called to his spokesman (Exo. 4:10-17)

Moses: depended largely on his brother Aaron (Exo. 4:10-17)

Moses: held the keys for the gathering of Israel (D&C 110:11)

Moses: established a kingdom of priest (Ex. 19, 28:1, 29:5 30:30, 40:12-15)

Moses: established the Passover and other ordinances under the authority of the Priesthood which he held.

Moses: led the migration from Egypt to (Ex.14)

Moses: Israel murmurs and complains many times about him (Ex. 16)

Joseph: apparently his linage goes back to Joseph of Egypt (2 Nephi 3)

Joseph: saw the Father and the Son and talked with them (JS-H 1:16-20)

Joseph: performed many signs and wonders with Zion's camp being a prime example (Church History Zion's Camp)

Joseph: organized the restored Church of Jesus Christ of Latter-Day Saints (D&C 107; 91-92)

Joseph: used the Urim & Thummin to translate the Book of Mormon (D&C 17:1)

Joseph: received revelation giving us The Book of Mormon, D&C, Pearl of Great Price.

Joseph: The Lord gave J.S. Sidney Rigdon as spokesman (2 Nephi 3:18; D&C 100:9-10)

Joseph: depended largely on his brother Hyrum (D&C 135:3)

Joseph: received the keys for the gathering of Israel from Moses in this dispensation (D&C 110:11)

Joseph: was ordained to the Aaronic Priesthood (C Hist. of C V1:179) Melchizedek Priesthood (D&C 84:21-28; 107:1, 3, 8,18)

Joseph: established the Sacrament and other ordinances under the authority of the Priesthood which he held (D&C 27:2)

Joseph: led the migration from New York to Ohio (C Hist. V1: 236)

Joseph: The Saints complain numerous times and some friends turned against him (Missouri Precautions, Ch XVI-XXVI)

Moses: established laws governing many aspects of life (Leviticus)

Joseph: taught proper principles and let the people govern themselves (statements by Joseph and Brigham)

Moses: plural marriage practiced in Old and New Test. (Gen 16:3-4; 25:1-2; 29:23-35; 4:1-6; 30: 3-4, 2 Samuel 12:6-7, Luke 13:28)

Joseph: part of "the restitution of all things" also included the reinstatement of plural marriage by the Lord (Acts 3:21; Isaiah;1-6) When abused (D&C 132:39; Jacob 2:26-30)

Moses: built the tabernacle under the direction of the Lord (ex. 25)

Joseph: built temples in Kirkland Oh. And Nauvoo II. (D&C 88; 109; W. Ceil McGavin, Nauvoo Temple)

Moses: was the head of his dispensation

Joseph: Moses in person appeared to Joseph and gave him the keys for the gathering of Israel in this dispensation (D&C 110:11-16)

Moses: could not go into the Promised Land (Deut. 34)

Joseph: was murdered in Carthage jail and couldn't lead the Saints to the Promised Land (Ch V6 page 612-622)

Moses: Pharaoh hardened his heart and would not let Israel go. He sent an army to stop them but the Lord intervened and parted the Red Sea which destroyed the army. (Exo. 14:5-30)

Joseph: President Poke decided not to let the Saints go and sent an army to stop them but the Lord intervened and froze the Mississippi solid so the army could not get to the Saints and stop them from leaving. (Nauvoo the Beautiful, by E Cecil Mc Gavi)

Brigham: called to lead the Saints to the Promised Land (introductory in Andrew Jenson, Church Chronology)

Joshua: called to lead Israel into the Promised Land (Joshua 1)

Joshua: led Israel through the Jordan River on dry ground (Josh. 3:13-17)

Brigham: the saints crossed the Mississippi river on ice, or dry land. The wagon train was about two miles long. (History of The Church of J. Jesus Christ of Latter-Day Saints, Vol. 7 Chapter 39)

4. Alma 30:44 – Alma said God uses the Earth and all things that are upon the face of it. He also uses signs and symbols to teach and testify.

The Savior taught using parables which included symbols such as "Pearl of Great Price" & "Lost Sheep" because those things are universal. With symbols, one doesn't need to be able to read in order to understand the message. For example:

Seattle Seahawks Football Team Logo   **Denver Broncos Football Team Logo**

In ancient times, when making a contract, the information would be written on a square clay tablet and stamped with a signet ring or other identifiable mark. Then, a corner would be a broke off. This became known as a covenant and restoration symbol. It was a covenant when the contract was made, and restored when the broken corner was replaced, when the contract was fulfilled. That is why it represents both covenant and restoration.

Covenant Symbol   **Restoration when broken corner is replaced**

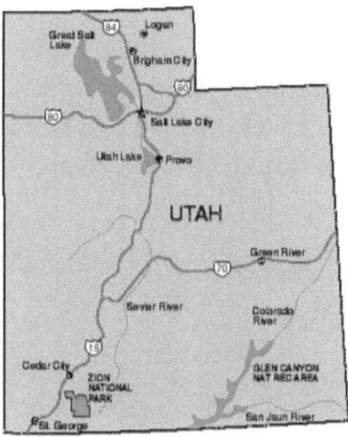

God shaped the State of Utah in the shape of the covenant symbol to show us He made a new covenant with us. God's signature or signet or stamp is a dead sea and there are only two places on earth where there is a dead sea.

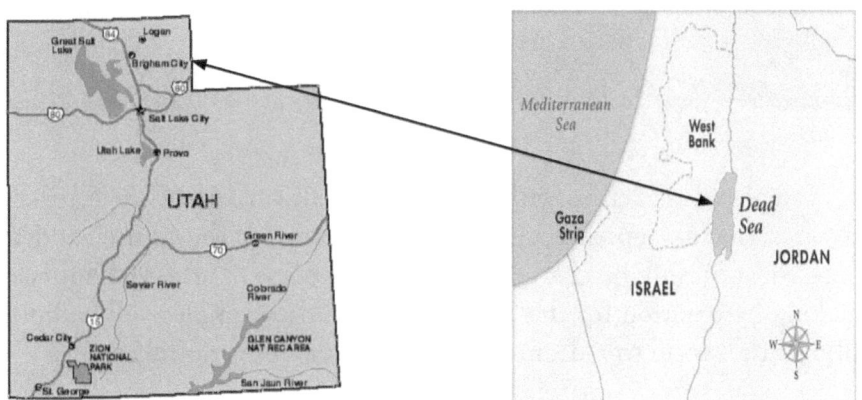

The Great Salt Lake is fed by the Jordan River   The Dead Sea is fed by the Jordan River

The stars also testify of Joseph. Revelation 12 describes a woman clothed with the sun and the moon at her feet and it is believed this is the constellation Virgo. It also says she has a crown of 12 stars. Leo is at her head but only has 9 stars. Usually in September, Mercury, Mars, and Venus enter this consultation of stars making 12 stars. Jupiter has been in retrograde in Virgo's womb for nine months and on September 23, 2017 Virgo, (The Christ Star) will leave the womb, thus fulfilling Revelation 12. This falls on Israel's Fall Gathering.

What has this to do with Joseph? Joseph was required to wait for four years before getting the golden plates. The day after he received the plates, the exact line up of the stars took place. Again, Sept. 23 was on the time where Israel celebrates their Fall Gathering. Joseph was charged with the gathering of Israel. Again this has only happened twice in 2000 years.

2017	**1827**
• Sept 23 – THE SIGN	• Sept 23 – THE SIGN
• Sept 22 – First Day of the New year (last day of Rosh Hashanah)	• Sept 22 – First Day of the New year (last day of Rosh Hashanah)
• Sept 21 – End of the 5777 year on the Jewish calendar. Last day of Elul	• Sept 21 – End of the 5587 year on the Jewish calendar. Last day of Elul
• Sept 20 – Rosh Hashanah begins in the evening	• Sept 20 – Rosh Hashanah begins in the evening

Now consider this:

Joseph was called to gather Israel from all corners of the Earth. I envision that on September 22, 2017 the prophet of the Church at that time will not only be charged with the gathering of all Israel but also making preparation for the Savior's return. Also, temples will be built all over the world to redeem the dead that are in the Spirit Prison.

Amos 3:7 Surely the Lord god will do nothing, but he revealeth his secret unto his servants the prophets.

Revelation 14:6 And I saw another angel fly in the midst of heaven, having the everlasting gospel to preach unto them that dwell on the earth, and to every nation, and kindred, and tongue, and people. We know this is the Angel Moroni.

Matthew 13:15 states, "This people's heart is waxed gross, and their ears are dull of hearing, and their eyes they have closed: lest at any time they should see with their eyes, and hear with their ears, and should understand with their heart, and should be convened, and I should heal them." 16: "But blessed are your eyes, for they see: and your ears, for they hear."

Joseph Smith was called of God to restore Christ's New Testament Church and complete the Covenant.

ABOUT THE AUTHOR

Donald Chadd has had a life-long interest in Native Amerian history and culture. When he was ten years old he found a handwritten book with a detailed history and illustrations of the Indians in the Four Corners area of Colorado and was fascinated by what he saw and read. He was determined to learn more. Over the years, Donald developed personal relationships with many Native Americans as both a miner in the uranium mines of Colorado and later as a registered representative for Prudential Financial in Cortez, Colorado. During his time with Prudential, Donald handled the insurance and retirement plans for the Adolescent Treatment Center in Shiprock, New Mexico. There he had the opportunity to converse with several of the elders of the Navajo tribe and was introduced to the many problems the youth were facing on the reservation. These experiences made a lasting impression on him and ultimately lead to the writing of this book.

In addition to his research and study of the Native American culture and his work as a financial advisor, Donald enjoyed raising German Shepherds which he donated to the military and teaching classes on the Constitution. He presently lives in the state of Washington with his wife and youngest daughter.

AFTERWORD

Additional information concerning ancient Native American history dating back to 2500 B.C. can be found in The Book of Mormon. You can get your FREE copy by calling 1-888-537-2200.

The information and conclusions in this book are not endorsed, sponsored by, or affiliated with The Church of Jesus Christ of Latter-day Saints or any other group or individua